dot zen 2.0

dot zen 2.0

On Marketing, Social Media, Technology, Public Relations, Human Capital & Leadership

Written by Seamus Phan
With contributions from Ter Hui Peng

Dot Zen 2.0 – On Marketing, Social Media, Technology, Public Relations, Human Capital & Leadership

ISBN–13: 978–0–9835058–1–5

Published by McGallen & Bolden Pte Ltd.

Text design by Seamus Phan, set in Calibri and Constantia.
Cover art from iStockphoto (Mark Wragg).

1. Leadership, strategy, entrepreneurship. 2. Human capital, human resource development. 3. Customer service, service quality, sales. 4. Branding, reputation management. 5. Marketing. 6. Public relations, publicity. 7. Social media, Internet, Web 2.0. 8. Mobile apps, audio, video, multimedia, interactive media. I. Phan, Seamus. II. Title.

987654321 Printed in the United States of America

Contents

With Gratitude...

This humble book project would not have been possible if not for the many field experiences we personally came across when consulting for clients, in a wide spectrum of projects and retained programs, from the decades we have behind us in running our practice, as well as our collective corporate experience before that.

On a personal level, we would like to thank our direct customers, friends we have met in the media through the decades, many business partners who labored with us to serve the needs of clients in events together, and the many people we met along the way, many of whom have become great friends. Many of these great people presented us with great opportunities to learn, to adapt what we know, to create and build new possibilities, and to be able to emerge with new insights, new perspectives, and new solutions.

It is a lifelong journey, and the journey may still be long. May all of you, whom we are blessed to know in our journeys, be blessed with joy, peace, and all that you wish for.

From Seamus...

As a publicist and journalist, one of the easiest ways to pen thoughts down quickly, is with a blog. I have been a blogger for a long time with only a short hiatus at one time. Writing casually on a blog is a great way to unwind, to crystalize thoughts, and to share ideas with like minds.

I was writing on my blog, inspired by the earlier success of our original paperback "Dot Zen," exploring various management areas that are relevant to an owner–manager like myself, and perhaps many others like me, as well as departmental practitioners in larger corporations. These broad areas include strategic leadership, human capital and development, customer service, branding and reputation, sales, marketing, public relations, social, audiovisual and mobile media. I believe these can benefit fellow owner–managers and practitioners, as we journey on in an ever–changing, ever–evolving business environment that melds previously distinct areas together.

Unlike the first book, this second rendition goes more hands–on, with more field–proven and tested tips and tricks we explored and used in our work. We include QR codes you can scan with your smartphone or tablet's camera to quickly surf and read the references, many of which we found useful and relevant.

Think of this book as a field and combat survival guide, something you scribble on, make "dog ears" on, and flip often. We hope you will use it often and show its battle scars of frequent use.

We live for the day, as life itself is transient and can change. We could be here today, and gone tomorrow. What is important is how we learn, adapt, and live to the fullest, contributing what we know and what we can to the fullest. The world can seem depressing when we choose to look at it that way, or the world can be exciting and stimulating to spur us on to greater heights and achieve greater things, when we choose to see its positives, and the positives we can bring to the world.

It is my sincere hope that we can all benefit from sharing our battle scars, our gray or white hairs, our tears, our laughter together. For we do not live alone, and we are part of a greater landscape, that each of us who is a single thread of distinctive designs, come together to form a complex and incredibly beautiful tapestry in life.

May your business journey be blessed with great joy, peace, strength and wisdom always.

Respectfully,

Seamus Phan
Fellow traveler

dot zen 2.0

Strategy & Leadership

Think startup, always

Every company goes through one of either scenarios: (1) Go belly up, or (2) become successful. If a company goes under, that's the end of the story for that company.

If a company becomes successful, again, it goes through one of either scenarios: (a) Remain successful for a long time, or (b) lose sight of success after some time and decays to oblivion.

No company is set up to fail right away, just as no employee is looking to fail at the job right after clinching the job. Every company, like every new employee, is looking to succeed. The trouble is, when a company reaches some degree of success, new people other than the founders are brought in, with diverse backgrounds, varied interests and passions, and sometimes, even divergent views and objectives.

When that happens, a company can begin to behave like a giant (it may be, or it may simply behave like one). That means longer, more tedious and sometimes counterproductive business processes that retard and sometimes trip up employees in doing their jobs well, or worse, retarding the growth of the company altogether, leading it to spiral dangerously downwards.

Therefore, at any stage of its existence, a company should always encourage a startup mentality and culture. Its people should always strive for courage, foresight, creativity, imagination, and of course, adhering to the same shared corporate vision and growth objectives.

Google, for example, is often cited as an exciting company of such characteristics – growing strong, and yet retaining the startup atmosphere.

Never be afraid to be nimble on your feet in chasing customers and markets, fast with your hands in seizing opportunities, and above all, retaining the bright spark in you that says, "I am an exciting startup," whatever the size of your company may be.

Retiring products and services – cutting off to thrive

We live in a world running at a breakneck speed today. Things that worked before, may not work anymore.

What do we do as businesses trying to keep pace with rapid changes? We become incisively decisive.

I read a great article from Jason Fried, cofounder and president of 37signals, LLC. I have admired the company since its earlier days and have been a loyal customer of their Basecamp SaaS "software as a service" (basecamp.com) for a long time, and still is.

In the article* featured on the very informational Inc. Magazine, Jason talked about the painful but necessary decisions the company made to retire perfectly profitable offerings such as Sortfolio and Writeboard as the company moves forward.

Jason is not alone in making such decisions, among many who run big and small businesses alike.

For example, in 2003, we took on an idea of becoming book publishers, representing small upstart authors. There were many fiction manuscripts submitted to us then for review, and quite frankly, besides the enormous work necessary to get these manuscripts ready for publishing, the stories were not compelling in the regional sense – that is, those stories might be compelling in their places of origins, but might not resonate with our side of the world. We did end up working with a few nonfiction authors, as book publicists, since publicity is our core business. We are not adverse to publicizing a great author with a ready and published book and has enough sponsorships and means to reach out to the market. We are not saying we will close the doors absolutely to every book manuscript, but unless there is a blockbuster–ready manuscript that is written exceptionally well, authors might be better served by a dedicated literary agent and publisher elsewhere.

Sometime in 2004, we were running our own mail servers as well as consulting for some clients then. Together with an old friend and Internet service provider (ISP), we codeveloped an anti–spam and anti–malware system for mail servers running on BSD servers (also capable of running on OS X and Linux). We even went so far as to register the trademark.

It was a great experiment and a great learning experience, but not sufficiently compelling enough for us to invest even more time and resources to commercialize it to a grand scale. If you ask us for advice and ideas, we would be more than happy to help you understand the technologies, but it would not be something we want to do full–time.

Therefore, fast forward to today, and our firm returned to focus on what we do best – communication.

We communicate our clients' ideas to the media and other stakeholders through holistic communications, whether it be public relations (PR), direct marketing, events, or even advertising (all types). We also help clients reach out to their audiences through social media, mobile and Web apps, which are more channels of communication.

We also leverage on our internal communication and human capital development expertise gained since the 1980s, to help clients develop their people through in–house learning programs.

As a small firm, it makes sense to focus on what we do best, given the resources and time we have on hand. It is an exciting world, and it may get even more exciting when reaching out to markets and customers through a variety of means.

Whatever the size of the organization, we need to always remember what we love best, and what we know best.

* http://www.inc.com/magazine/201207/jason–fried/when–to–kill–a–product.html

Paradox of the "last mover" advantage

We often hear of the first mover's advantage in business and marketing, but not every first mover ends up the winner. There may be wisdom in not being the first, and having stamina and discernment instead.

For example, if we scour the news, it is not difficult to find big corporations and even governments, making mistakes that are sometimes colossal.

Mistakes are not abnormal, since we are merely human. The important thing therefore, is making strategic recoveries from the mistakes expediently and with as little further financial and other dents as possible. In the heydays of the dot—com era, the idea of being the first mover being the winner was the war cry of the day then. Every startup was rushing to be first in a niche or specific area of technology and innovation.

Some years later, the dot—com era went under, replaced by more financial woes worldwide, and the age of discernment, responsibility and accountability began to kick in.

Now so many years later, we are still cautious about the near and farther future. It is no longer a "sure—win" to simply copy or emulate past successful models or businesses. What we need to do is to step back and examine all possibilities and outcomes, and discern with wisdom, rather than mere bravado.

I once read a "wu xia" (martial arts) story by a famous author. From vague memory, the subplot was about 8 grandmasters of martial arts, who met at the summit of a mountain to compete and compare their skills with each other. Every time they met, all of them were equally skilled and no one won. Eventually, they decided that the only winner was simply, the last man living to the oldest age possible.

As was said, the meek shall inherit the world. Therefore, there is nothing wrong by being slow, or last movers. When every rash entity has fallen, and the dust has settled, being slow or being last, simply means you are the surviving one.

4 marks of a true leader

I was flipping through magazines, and some of these thoughts converged on my mind.

True leaders may be gifted with exceptional qualities, but it is how they work collaboratively with their people that make great things happen. What kinds of leaders inspire us to do more, to scale greater heights, to conquer great challenges that frighten most people?

1. **He is with me**

   Would you follow a leader who hides away from challenges, and not face up to the same challenge you face? When you confront difficult terrains and challenges daily, would you prefer a leader who merely encourage you with empty words? Or would you rather serve with a leader who dares to roll up sleeves and get to work alongside with you, fighting business challenges together?

2. **He learns, and I learn**

   In a fast–changing world today, yesterday's knowledge may become obsolete today, or at most, a short while thereafter. When we stop learning, we become terribly stagnant and soon, we will be useless to the business environment we operate in. Every day is a new learning challenge, a new learning opportunity. We must embrace learning as a habit, and as a passion. Therefore, would you follow a leader who holds perilously on to antiquated knowledge that may have little semblance to reality now and have little applications in the business landscape? Or would you rather follow a leader who keeps pace with you in learning, or even ahead of you so that you can always benefit from his insights and knowledge?

3. He does not need "yes" men

All too often, communities within a business environment becomes stagnant not only with the lack of learning, but also with people who are more interested in self–preservation than in truly contributing to the growth of the business entity. In short, too many "yes" men who rally behind leaders, offering no real help, and no real growth for the company. Would you rather work with a leader who prefers to gather a group of "yes" men to echo his own thoughts and ways? Or would you rather work with a leader who gathers a varied team of people which brings varied experiences, complementary knowledge, and creative inputs to the table?

4. He has courage as his middle name

A leader is someone we look up to, to make difficult decisions when we dare not, or would not. The leader cannot be a symbol of fear. The leader must be a symbol of strength, integrity, fortitude, and courage. When things get tough, he is in front of us to take the heat. When things look impossible, he encourages us forward, with him in front as our shield. Would you follow a leader who leaves us in the lurch when trouble hits shore? Or would you rather follow a leader who takes all blame, cedes all praise to our efforts (however humble), and is someone we can instinctively lean on during challenging times? The business world is getting tougher, and we need leaders of steel. We can all do with more inspiration at our business battlegrounds.

Flying the entrepreneurial flag

It is not easy to study in school these days. It is difficult to work in a competitive workplace today. It is even more difficult to set up shop. So why do it?

I enjoy the clean taste of Espresso or Caffè Americano, without the trappings of chocolate, milk or sugar to cloud my enjoyment of just black coffee. Call me a purist, or maybe just a middle–aged guy watching his waistline.

I frequent a café (part of a regional chain) often, simply because their front–line managers are friendly and welcoming, and the coffee rather decent. Mind you, their coffee offerings aren't cheap if you compare to the neighboring hawker center, but you get a friendly atmosphere to relax and take a break in.

One of their managers recently offered me a taste of 2 of his own blends – Espresso style. I was curious why he did that. I tasted them and they were smooth, with a pleasant fragrance, and no roughness whatsoever.

He told me his desire to start his own café, and these were his own research and blends. He sought my opinion to compare the standard café blends with his, and described just how he created his own blends.

I meet many people in my course of work as a keynote speaker and facilitator. There are many people, young and old alike, who at some point have told me they want to start a café or something related to food and drinks.

Invariably, my question to them was, "Do you know how to cook or handle the operations of the food business?" Almost 100% of the time, the answer was "no, but I will employ people who know how to."

I am unconvinced you can be an entrepreneur unless you know the nuts and bolts of the business.

Even Mr Warren Buffett would often only invest in businesses he could understand, and that is wise indeed. Should there be problems in a business, and there will be plenty when running one, the owner–manager would at least have some knowledge of fixing the problems, or have the field experience to work with people to solve those problems together.

Flying the entrepreneurial flag is the ultimate frontier of the business arena. It takes guts, perseverance, humility, continuous learning, and most of all, passion.

Those who believe in making a quick buck and then make a quick exit, invariably fail quickly because they lack the fundamental attributes.

We toast to you, fellow entrepreneurs flying the flag high, we salute you who put in blood and sweat in all that you do, and may you enjoy continued success in this turbulent world.

Do you know why CEOs learn software programming?

I was reading an article about CEOs who see the benefit of understanding and even learning programming languages. Why would or should they?

Imagine a new restaurant. Although one can certainly open a restaurant without becoming a chef, or even knowing how to cook anything, it certainly is a great benefit to know how to. Imagine your executive chef quitting on you, leaving you with just a few kitchen helpers, in the busiest day of the week, and customers are queuing in a long line. What can you do?

If you are a good chef, such a situation would not derail you. You roll up your sleeves, put on a clean apron, and get to cook. The show goes on, and your customers are happy.

In the world of information technology and social media today, chief executives would do themselves a great favor if they know the lingo and the mechanics behind the inner workings of the social media and technology world.

They do not need to roll up sleeves and take excessive caffeine to program in code, but having a decent understanding of programming languages, databases, servers, operating systems, etc, would empower them to talk with their internal information technology and development teams better, and certainly would understand if technology projects are in good progress, or stalled. Clearly there are many benefits.

In today's world, knowing how to code for a CEO is akin to expecting the same person to know enough about finance, manufacturing, quality control, etc.

So, the next time you are in an airport waiting for your flight, in a business networking event, or perhaps attending a symposium, don't be surprised if you meet a CEO, or many CEOs, who can code. These peers of yours might just be the norm very soon.

Are you a maybe, or a has been?

Some individuals or institutions may sing praises about past glories and track records, but it may appear there is more persuasion to potential rather than historical successes.

In an interesting article* that talked about Professor Tormala and his team's study of how potential may be more compelling than reality when it comes to decision–making, we realize that how we arrive at decisions are not necessarily a mathematical or logical decision. I would tend to agree. I too, fall prey to simply presenting my extensive experience and skills to employers (when I was an employee) and to clients (as a consultant) alike.

After all, the comfort of knowing what has been accomplished, seems to resonate with many people, including myself. Increasingly, that is no longer the case.

When we are helping clients scout for talents, or when we are looking for people for our business, we tend to evaluate the person based on what we perceive as mere potential, rather than desiring to find "track records." There are many reasons, but let us name two.

1. We have observed some experienced people also packing along baggage of obstinate complacency, doing particular roles with dated methods simply because it seems easy, rather than thinking hard and creatively to arrive at new ways to tackle problems and challenges.

2. With experience, some people tend to begin to inflate their egos, beyond their levels of competency and potential. The result is that there may be professional conflict, which in a tightly knit team, will be undesirable for team leaders to have to deal with. A collegial team putting all their creativity and talents together to help solve problems, is much more desired than prima donnas on the downhill. Those without experience, but with enthusiasm, curiosity, tenacity, commitment, professionalism, and humility, would be far more valued in my opinion, because I can develop these emerging talents and help them reach their full potential, while they would also be able to play well in a tightly knit team to reach joint objectives for clients.

It is not difficult to find spectacular failures where people of extensive track records were put into incompatible roles when we look around. It is an increasingly complex world and there are complex scenarios that demand humility, continuous learning, and a capacity to adapt to changing scenarios. Clients demand new ideas, new methods, new processes, to tackle ever–changing business problems and even old problems tired of old solutions.

Having a person with enough humility to be an empty cup desiring to be filled, is far more desirable than a cup previously filled with no room to spare. Being a person who is a "positive maybe" is much better in today's world than a "has been."

* http://www.influenceatwork.com/potential–or–reality–when–it–comes–to–influencing–others–whats–more–persuasive/

You may just meet your doppelgänger

Have you met someone who looks just like you? Just like our ideas are not that unique most of the time, despite our own pride. What do we do despite having fierce and similar competition?

I went to a recently opened café on a Saturday morning and was greeted by the friendly manager. The manager looked at me and said he saw me at a gym downtown. I said that I was not there. He kept saying he saw me there just an hour earlier.

The truth was, I was never there, and have not been a member of that particular gym network for nearly a decade, and I was certainly not even downtown in the same morning. I was home and in bed before I was at the café in the business district.

That was not the first time something like this happened to me. When I was much younger, someone commented they saw me in a disco one night. The reality was I was never there, and I was home as usual (I am not a night person). When I was much older, someone called me by a different name, and I was certainly not that person.

Therefore, the logical reason is that someone out there looks very much like me, or could even be a dead ringer for me. I am not arrogant enough to imagine my looks are that unique (my fingerprints might be, but my looks are not). The legend of the Doppelgänger is age–old, which means "double goer" in German. These days, it just means having someone out there who look just like us.

What do Doppelgängers mean to us in business and marketing?

Ideas are not that unique, because many similar ideas and expressions can coexist, developed independently, having similar functionality, and even look–and–feel. Rather than imagining that we must fight tooth and nail over the straws of originality we imagine, we as business leaders and marketers must simply move on, and fast forward.

1. **Ideas can become dated** when the time is over. We have created an effective marketing and promotional campaign some years earlier for a client. The campaign was a resounding success. However, a few years later, the client decided to rehash the same idea with a different wrapper. Unfortunately, the climate has changed and consumers were no longer interested in long, tedious promotions. We advised the client against such an idea even if it worked the first time.

2. We must **keep abreast of trends** even if we are leaders today. If there is a particular trend, whether it be fashion, food, technology, or media, this trend will not last. This has been proven often. We must innovate, invent, reinvent, and go back and revisit the drawing board all too often with gusto and passion. Time waits for no one, and certainly, the marketplace and our competition would not wait for us too.

3. Let us put our ears to the ground and **listen hard**. What real needs are consumers seeking (rather than mere desires)? What are their pain points and challenges? What would make their lives better? The best inventions, the best technologies, the best products, are often those that serve real needs, solve real problems, and work simply and confidently,

without putting hoops and hoops to confound our consumers.

Be not afraid of Doppelgängers, but rather, of our own inaction and inability to move on and forward, to invent and innovate. Spend more time listening to the ground, spend more time hard at work to create and refine, and spend less time looking back and biting others. Those who lead and those who win, look confidently to the fore.

Liberate our inner child to creative and innovative fruition

What do the greatest minds such as Sir Isaac Newton, Leonardo Da Vinci, Dr. Albert Einstein, Nikola Tesla, and many others, have in common – genius aside?

I was watching my little 5–year–old nephew and niece (they are fraternal twins) becoming so animated over a simple spinning top (and so thankfully not over a tablet or computer game). The beautiful child in both of them brought out the best of their joys, and much more, much of the optimistic creativity in both of them when they learn, draw and even dance.

Increasingly, we see structured learning programs designed for the young, to the mature audiences at the workplace, that aim to conform and confine minds into pigeon holes. Yes, there are parallel streams that aim to delineate people, hopefully to bring out the innate brilliance in many people, but these programs are far fewer than many "mainstream" programs that pump loads of information into growing and working minds of today.

Yet, we have seen, through the annals of human history, many of the most brilliant minds who managed to put thoughts and hearts to action, who are not conformists confined and contorted into tiny slots and holes.

So what do we see in Leonardo Da Vinci, Dr. Albert Einstein, Nikola Tesla, Sir Isaac Newton, and many other great minds?

Their brilliance is clear and well documented, whether archived in respected journals, engraved onto stone walls, or embedded deep into gears and machinery that power many things today. And more, what differentiates these brilliant minds from many others, is simply that they were willing to let the "child" take center–stage.

One great marketing mind, the late Mr. Steve Jobs of Apple, Pixar and NeXT fame, once spoke to students at the prestigious Stanford University on June 12, 2005, to "stay young, stay foolish." Those were powerful words that still resonate today.

The greatest minds start young. The greatest minds remain young. There is no greater spring or fount of creativity and innovation than that of a naive, curious, and eager childlike mind, whether in a little child's body, or a much older one. Stay young, think positive, and the pearl of creativity and invention will grow within you.

Expensive? Yes. Flawless? No.

Even as business climates are competitive, there is no good and sensible reason to succumb to every customer demand, especially if it is unreasonable and based on fallacies.

Recently, I read on a social media post, of a customer who bought a fashion item, and claimed that just with one single use, the item was damaged. She went back to the store, demanding a one–for–one exchange, claiming that given the high price of the item, it should not spoil so easily.

Sounds reasonable? Maybe ... until you see the flawed argument and fallacy.

First, the evidence from the photograph she posted online showed that the item was damaged through either: (1) an accident, or (2) an intentional damage.

Here's the fallacy of her argument, that if an item costs so much, it should not spoil easily. This brings to mind, many fragile items on the market today, that would cost a great deal of money, that would not be covered under any exchange or refund due to an abuse of the item by a customer.

For example, if a customer bought an expensive silk dress that carried instructions that it must be dry–cleaned under low heat, then if the customer accidentally or willfully subject the silk dress to a washing cycle, there is no recourse.

Likewise, if out of a fit of anger, a customer destroys an expensive laptop with a hammer, the evidence will prevent a vendor from exchanging a good laptop with the willfully damaged one.

Why is there such an aftermarket space for accessories for smartphones, laptops, automobiles and so on?

For example, when you buy an expensive smartphone, you may then buy a screen protector, and a protective casing, so that that expensive smartphone would be better protected from daily use (and misuse or abuse).

Likewise, when you buy an expensive laptop, you may buy a good quality laptop bag that offers adequate padding and protection for your spanking new laptop.

Automobiles also enjoy tremendous add–ons, with owners protecting the interiors, the exteriors, the innards (engine), and so on, just so that the wear and tear of daily use of the automobiles will not wear out the automobiles sooner than the owners hope.

Fashion items also demand delicate care for them to reduce the effects of wear and tear.

Many product warranties carry extensive terms and conditions, especially when it comes to care of the product, and how it is handled. Products may carry extended warranties that offer greater protection (including accidental damage), but only as a paid premium warranty.

Out of 100 customers, most customers would have simple desires and demands that would meet fairly and squarely with the deliverables and performance of the suppliers and vendors.

In short, most customers and suppliers or vendors have mutual respect for each other to know the terms and conditions of a product. A small number of customers and their complaints can receive adequate resolution and relationships maintained.

But there will always be a very, very small number of customers who will never benefit from a respectful service relationship, and may be toxic to managing our fragile front–line workforce. When we approach a public servant to help us with something, we have to be respectful when making any request, and have to be reasonable too. Expect the same in any human relationship, whether it be in customer service, or even in a family relationship. The same rules apply.

Think of the fable of the princess and the pea. If you have a princess, you certainly won't expect the princess to take abuse from anyone or anything.

Likewise, because a product is very expensive, it might also carry many conditions to caring for it. Remember, the (paying) customer is not always right. The simplest and wisest way, is to respect every customer (paying, internal, suppliers, etc), with the most committed delivery you can provide.

Success comes through the long–form

How many times have we seen success? How does it look like? Is it something that can be achieved overnight AND be sustainable?

Life is a meandering path, a long marathon, a journey of many turns and corners that demands all of our might and fortitude till the end. Life is never about a moment of glory only, but how we struggle and strive through the whole journey till our last breath. It is about the entire journey and how it changes us for the better till the end, and not little pockets of vainglory.

When I was a teenager, I was an artist. I enrolled in art college (the youngest student in that program in that old art school then) to learn Chinese Brush Painting.

The teacher was an interesting gentleman, having been a teacher in the college for a long time. There are 2 forms of Chinese brush painting – "gong bi" (the fine–stroked approach), and the "xie yi" (the rough brush strokes approach). This teacher would teach us both techniques, although each of us would find inclinations towards one approach rather than the other, or both.

The teacher would have us copy paintings he has done before, as copying paintings is one of the entry–level methods of teaching Chinese brush painting. We would copy many of his paintings laboriously, in "xie yi" and "gong bi" strokes, from themes ranging from nature, flora, fauna, people, and still life.

My nature is more free–spirited, and naturally, I would gravitate towards the "xie yi" style of painting. I did not like the "gong bi" method at all, which to me then, was a style of painting that pales in comparison to the "xie yi" method – which IMHO, is full of energy, raw and powerful, compared to the fine strokes of "gong bi", which can seem lifeless and merely technical. Still, I had to laboriously put in effort to recreate the "gong bi" paintings on my own, against my personal preferences.

Then came a time when we were nearing graduation, and the teacher told all of us who remained, that he would carve a name seal for each of us. A name seal is usually a small marble (or similar) block, with the name of the person carved out in the underside. The seal would be pressed against the seal paste (usually red), and then stamped on Chinese calligraphy and paintings as a proof of the identity of the artist.

There are 2 methods of carving a name seal: (1) Carve the name out of the surface, which is infinitely easier, or (2) Carve the surface surrounding the name out, which demands a lot more out of the seal carver.

harder   easier

The teacher opted for the easier method of carving the name out of the surface, which is perfectly fine. But what annoyed me was what he did to my name.

My Chinese name has 3 characters, the last character is pronounced as "jia–1" (the first tone). The characters in the Chinese language often confound some foreigners when learning the language, because many characters are pronounced in different tones, and a flat or mispronounced tone may render the contextual meaning of the spoken word differently. Also, there are many characters with the same tone, even if the actual character is completely different, and have different meanings.

right   wrong

The teacher carved my last character "jia–1" with a completely different character with the same sound, simply because the character he chose had very few strokes and so was easier to carve. But it would mean that what he carved was NOT my name at all. He knew that he intentionally chose that character, and not out of ignorance, and that annoyed me then because he as a teacher, always told us never to take short cuts, and that every stroke has to be dutifully copied and learned. To a young child, this hypocritical behavior was unacceptable.

In life, when you trace the path of history, you would immediately realize, that many of the greatest minds, whether they be artists, musicians, scientists, or inventors, have labored with their heart and soul, for what they believed in. No success, especially if it is sustainable till the end, can be achieved without putting in one's whole being into it, completely, until the last breath. History is the best judge of that.

Human Capital
& Development

The best marketing people

In almost any contemporary business, there is a need for a marketing team.

It could be a team of one, or a large international team managing campaigns and programs in different languages, different marketing channels, to different audiences.

In the social media world we live in today, it is no longer sufficient for marketing executives to be talking about print and broadcast campaigns.

Executives are now looking for marketing people with the courage, the creativity, the knowledge, and the field–tested experience to put together marketing programs and campaigns that drive the brand message to print, broadcast, and digital (in the fullest sense of the word).

Marketers must have courage, especially the courage to dream big, to dream far ahead in the future, and to dream boldly. In the world of "me too" products and services, what differentiates one company from the next is mindshare of the customers. And mindshare is an increasingly tough and fluid quality to gain and retain.

Marketers need creativity to propel the company's brand, products and services forward. Marketers may not and often should not be the actual people doing graphic design or video editing (even if some actual knowledge can help in bridging project management), but should have the creativity to dream up dramatic, attractive and viral campaigns, especially on the social media platforms.

Marketers need knowledge, and not just bits and pieces, and not incomprehensible volumes of raw data. Raw data is useless for marketing until they are properly distilled into usable knowledge the marketer and his corporate team can use to succeed in the marketplace and win customers. This also means a good marketer cannot be in a cocoon with no outside knowledge. He should be one who is a voracious reader who devours information quickly, efficiently, and productively. Think and act like a shark.

Marketers need real experience. It is easy for someone to dream big and dream fancifully, but can such ideas be actually deployed in the field?

For example, when a marketer forwards huge, gigabyte–sized image files for print is a sure way of telling us that real experience in print production is missing. After all, you need to understand what the practical production requirements of a typical print advertisement are.

Likewise, not optimizing video files down to digestible sizes for streaming on the Internet implies a lack of hands–on knowledge about the mechanics of video formats, usable sizes, and Internet delivery.

Therefore, again, read widely, try frequently, and gain actual usable experience that can streamline your marketing campaigns for maximum effectiveness with the least deployment challenges.

The roulette of individual skills

Often, we imagine that the brand name lends some "aura" of protection against lapses in customer service. The reality is that each of our front–liners matter in customer engagements.

I don't go for expensive haircuts, but would rather go for the fixed price barbers that are all over the island. These barber shops are convenient, clean, and you get a decent haircut rather quickly.

Most of the time, I would frequent a particular branch of the chain, and most of the time, there are a few familiar barbers there who would cut my hair efficiently with cordial conversations. However, the last time I went to the barber, I was attended to by a new barber, who did not seem to have the prerequisite skills of her peers in the same shop.

My scalp suffered some knocks and scratches due to her inexperience. At the end of the haircut, I could visibly see irregularities in my hairline and overall haircut, but I am perhaps too lazy to ask her to correct the badly done haircut. On top of that, she did not seem to be in a good mood either (it is not an easy job, I understand).

Today, I went to the same shop, and there were two barbers. One of them was a familiar face who has attended to my haircuts often, and the other, the lady who cut my hair badly the last time. I prayed that I would get the older lady who seemed to be familiar with my needs, and luckily enough, she attended to me.

At the end of the haircut, I got what I needed: Efficiency, a good cut, and pleasant chitchat that made the already fast haircut, even more pleasant.

Therefore, when we examine a service business, it is very different from a retail business selling tangible, physical products. A service business such as a barber, relies on the individual skills and talents of each front–liner.

A service business is not about bringing out products from shelves and punching in numbers on a cash register. A service business needs to engage the very best of front–line crew, so that each customer can have not just the best possible service, but a repeatable level of service standards that the customer would come to expect and love.

It is certainly not easy, as the work ethic, attitude, and aptitude of each employee will be different, and maintaining consistent and repeatable service quality will make much more demands on a service business compared to a simple retail business selling physical products.

Remember, our customers rely on our consistency, and not just good service quality, that would place as little stress on them whenever they visit our service outlets. It should not be a roulette driven by chance, but a dependable machinery scrupulously watched over by quality managers.

2 simple attributes of a good staffer or partner

What is your stance of filling a position in your company? Getting a person you really need and want? Or fill the position and hope for the best?

If you have, like me worked in a large manufacturing concern before, you would appreciate the challenges a human resource executive would have.

On one hand, the line people are pressing you to fill jobs. On the other hand, you may not find suitable and qualified candidates to fill those jobs. What would you do?

Some might simply resort to filling the jobs with whatever candidates come by. This might pacify the line colleagues initially, but then the candidates weren't suitable to begin with, and turnover occurs, often more than necessary. The result is that nobody is pacified.

I am of the belief that in today's context, it is probably better for everyone (the company, the human resource team, the line folks, and the candidates), that only the right candidates are recruited for the particular jobs.

It would certainly reduce turnover because the right candidate is recruited for the right job, and would reduce staff turnover over the long haul.

If there aren't candidates that fit the job, I would recommend waiting rather than recruiting anybody and then realizing you may have to let the person go very soon.

It is certainly no walk in the park to find the right candidates. Who would be the right candidates for a particular job?

Two things come to mind – attitude and aptitude.

Aptitude for a particular job may refer to competency to perform at a certain level. There are many candidates to choose from these days. For most jobs, some kind of prerequisites must be fulfilled.

For example, some jobs have field experience requirements. You can't operate on someone unless you are trained as a surgeon, and have done sufficient hours in a hospital. Some jobs make technical demands on a person. You can't be a combat commando or a naval diver if you don't have the prerequisite fitness levels. Some jobs demand dexterity, knowledge, mental reflexes, and so on, all of which must be met before the candidates can be considered for shortlisting.

Having considered all these, attitude is important too, and perhaps even more important for entry–level or particular professions.

I remember fondly, when I was recruited for a banking job in the 1980s, the vice president who headhunted me said that academic qualifications weren't all that important, and that it is the potential and the attitude of the person that would make the difference.

If you are hungry to succeed and perform at a job, you would make every effort to learn fast and voraciously, work harder than others, and be committed to making contributions to the company. Contrast this person with someone with all the qualifications, but no desire to work hard or learn.

Filling a position should not be a trivial decision. Treat it like a serious relationship you hope to develop for the long term. The candidate whom you hire, will appreciate that he or she is the right candidate and would also hope to work with you for the long haul.

Tenure and youth – there is no shortcut

I am a fan of the Mad Men series, a TV series about an advertising agency set against the backdrop of the 1960s.

I was watching an episode when lead character, Don Draper, the creative director, scolded Peggy, a copywriter, over her overzealous pursuit of recognition. Fiction mimics life. It happens everyday in real life too.

There is no shortcut to recognition if you lack experience.

Look around us, and it is not difficult to find many organizations populated with very young management running them. There is nothing wrong, except that experience is something that can only come through decades of labor and pains, frequent meeting of failures and conquering them.

Sure, talents may abound in the young, but talents are not privy only to the young. The older predecessors do not lack talent, and some may very well be much better than the young. Technology can be an enabler for the young and it may appear that the young seems more nimble and quick in their work, but the reality may not be so. Many of the older executives who are keeping pace with technology, have no trouble outperforming the younger peers simply because they have decades of field and battleground experience to tap on at the speed of thought.

I have observed some young people who become complacent and lethargic at their work, believing that their skills and talents are under–appreciated. However, merely doing the same tasks repeatedly, without putting in more effort, more learning, more enthusiasm, and more participation with team members, do not make the hours clocked any more valuable to managers or the businesses.

Conversely, I have also observed some young people whom I admire and respect a great deal and would gladly recommend them for work. The most appreciated young executives are often those who are extremely hardworking, optimistic and cheerful, respectful of leaders and peers, eager learners, and cooperative to make every peg and nut in the corporate machinery work for the macro objectives of the organization.

No talent is indispensable, if the person insists on behaving like an out–of–sorts prima donna with no respect or regard for fellow team mates. The bright and successful young executives are often humble and respect knowledge and experience, and are eager to absorb the tenured experience of their older counterparts.

A word of caution for us who are older executives too. Just because we have tenure and field experience, do not make us immune to the transient and rapidly changing business environments. We need to learn constantly and to improve our expertise and skills as much as the young.

In the world of computing, we too, must keep abreast with what the young finds as second nature.

Like the fictional character Draper in Mad Men commented, I would concur that every need for recognition, must be tempered by real field experience, and over time.

The crux has to be in a person who is positive, eagerly learning, committed, and patient. I applaud those younger ones who are positive and humble, and who have continuously aligned themselves with the macro objectives, realizing that without the organization and the team, their own ground is but hollow.

Life is as much what you put in more upfront for the benefit of others, than what you expect out of it without putting in anything, or much at all.

Structured or unstructured learning at the workplace?

When I was developing networked and computer–based learning in the 1980s, the writing was already on the wall, that self–directed learning will become a mainstay at the workplace.

Today, in the twenty–first century, that still rings true. As a human resource development (HRD) practitioner, I must confess I too would be tempted to prefer structured learning where I can easily get something designed, developed, tested in the workplace, and audited. Such programs are more easily "sold" to corporate management, with finite timelines and measurable values that leaders can easily grapple with.

However, the modern workplace demands much more unstructured learning. Many companies are now no longer passive and reactive to the rapidly changing global economies and the market conditions, and prefer to take more active roles in not just adapting to economic and market forces, but to attempt to stay ahead of the curve.

This means that some structured learning programs face immediate obsolescence once they are developed. Corporate knowledge has evolved to a real–time beast that does not stop, but keeps changing, sometimes drastically.

The emerging generation of workers these days have shorter attention spans, and are not afraid to speak up, or even walk out. They would often attempt to multitask (or more correctly, rapid sequential processing of segments of tasks), toying with their smartphones, tablets, and desktop computers.

Structured learning programs in corporate classrooms would often bore such workers, and yield less than desired learning results, compared to workers of yesteryears. What would be unstructured learning methods at the workplace?

Social networking is a current paradigm that most modern workers are already familiar with. Unstructured learning can be adapted to be informal and real–time, tapping on micro–blogs, and social media networks such as Facebook, Google+ or Twitter, or even video–based platforms such as YouTube, Vimeo or self–hosted video platforms. The method to deliver learning should be bite–sized, entertaining, and intriguing, to engage the younger workers. These staffers are also more vocal, and such informal learning platforms' built–in commenting systems become yet another informal learning and sharing channel.

Other on–demand learning tools would include the more established platforms such as video and audio podcasting, probably within the corporate networks. Another common platform are "Webinars," which may combine recorded audios, videos, presentation slides, and annotations.

When workers progress in their responsibilities and seniority, unstructured learning can also include mentoring by established and respected internal and external experts. Classroom–based learning require many employees and managers sitting in the same room at the same time, which can be resource–intensive, and challenging in today's fast–paced workplace. Unstructured learning can quickly adapt to individualized and self–directed learning, which are great ways for the mobile and emerging workforce to learn from.

Old grandma and disciplined hard work

I was watching a Taiwanese travel program on cable TV, and the host chatted with an old grandma he met on the train, who religiously traveled every day for 50 years to buy daily groceries for her family. What can we learn from her?

When was the last time you boarded a slow train and savor the journey? Today, we may fly on airliners to distant locations, or travel by mass transit rail systems and even high–speed rail systems, or perhaps travel to various city locations by taxi cabs. Yet, there is something nostalgic about riding a train.

The TV host boarded the first train at the station, 5.10 AM to be exact. It was pitch dark, and the host went into the cabin and saw a few passengers. He sat down besides a serene old grandma with an empty grocery basket and an umbrella. The old grandma was probably in her seventies, and had a serene and benign smile that showed no signs of her difficult early life. She was given away by her birth family at an early age, but through hard work and discipline, her children and grandchildren are all successful and happy.

Yet, for the past 50 years, she woke up every day at 4.30 AM (except Mondays), to travel from her small town to the train station, took the train to a transit bus station, then took a bus to the market to buy groceries. All out of a labor of love for her family. Even as her gait was slow and slightly limp, you could only find a serene joy when you look at her.

In the fast–paced world today, all too often at our workplace, we find some younger people ranting about the difficulties of their lives on their social media channels and blogs. Do a random read, and you may likely find writings on material buys, relationships, jobs, and so on. Sadly, there are very few such online writings that tell us about fighting and conquering challenges in life with a smile fueled by an inner strength, that would inspire and transfigure us when we read them.

We can all surely do with more inspiration, more motivation, more spirit, and more heart. We can all learn from the old grandma who religiously traveled to and fro from home for the past 50 years to buy food for her family, with discipline, with inner strength, and with love.

No one is an expert, but experience counts

Recently, a social media practitioner mentioned that no one is really an expert in social media. True, except that gray or white hair does matter in every industry, especially in marketing and branding.

I read a great story of Mr. Michael Zone, 90 years young, who graduated with a high school diploma on December 8, 2011*.

And in 2009, Ms. Gennie Kocourek, 53 years young then, graduated with a medical degree**.

These are just 2 stories out of many similar stories, of inspirational people who braved advancing years, to earn knowledge through mainstream and nontraditional means.

Clearly, age is never the impediment to gaining knowledge. Conversely, a clean slate is just that – clean. You can be brilliant, but without the prerequisite experience gained from the battlefield of life and its many turns, you would clearly lack the same insights and depth of someone much older, who has been here and done that.

So yes, no one can be truly an expert or a "guru" in many of the contemporary technological fields, since areas such as social media, is fluidly evolving, with new technologies being launched, existing technologies or companies going away, technologies being acquired and repositioned, and so on.

The competition for similar technologies is fierce, with stalwarts fighting tooth and nail with new entrants. There is no standstill, with practitioners like us go on learning and laboring, every day.

When you look for a social media practitioner, remember that social media is merely a technology enabler. It is not a business tool that delivers results by itself. You need practitioners who have sufficient gray and white hair behind them to understand business dynamics, the psychology of people, and business processes, and perhaps even the various geographical sensitivities, to help you gauge the best way forward.

Just having a social media account would be pointless in delivering business results if you don't have an advisor who can bring to you business, marketing and branding expertise and experience gained from the real battlefields out there.

So, while all of us are learners every day, we recognize real world experience is what can help transform our businesses forward, marrying technologies with real world demands.

*Source: http://www.lasvegassun.com/news/2011/dec/09/90–year–old–veteran–high–school–graduation–caps–li/

**Source: http://www.med.wisc.edu/news–events/news/gennie–kocourek–a–new–md–at–age–53/898

Learning + Laboring = Life

Unemployment is affecting many places and many people. I was watching a Taiwanese cable TV program just now, and the panelists were debating the issue of career challenges and unemployment.

One of the guests on the show was a former gas delivery person who lost his home and everything else in a natural disaster. Did he become desolate and simply give up? No! He is now a hardworking local tour guide after going through retraining, and now earns a decent salary and gets commission during peak tour seasons working overtime.

Another guest on the show was a mother with a visually challenged son. A few parents with similarly challenged kids got together, formed a self–help group, and today has a thriving online business selling piano tuning services to schools and other entities. The mothers are the salespersons, empowering themselves with a new career while looking after the interests of their kids.

A guest on the show commented that many young people have unreal pay expectations these days, and said that some young graduates are even asking for NT100,000 per month for their first job (around US$3,400)! Of course, they remained jobless. The typical pay for a fresh graduate there is probably closer to NT30,000 per month (around US$1,000).

And another guest mentioned that every person, especially those in their thirties and older have to keep learning, because continuous learning is the ONLY way to justify any pay increase, or to get a job even during economic depression. One example quoted by the guest on the show was a person who worked very hard on the job, and on the side, earned 8 vocational certificates. This hardworking person eventually earned a home and went to Japan for further studies.

There is no stopping in life. There is no luxury of lazing back. You keep moving. You pace yourself, so that you don't burn out. Life is a marathon that lasts as long as you are alive.

My grandfather, whom I admire a great deal, was a former brigadier general who later became a professor of economics. He kept working, teaching, writing, and publishing his works, even when he reached his nineties. He is ninety–eight this year.

My dad, in his seventies, kept learning as well. He can use the Mac and even do data entry in Chinese, plus many other things he learned, and still keeps learning everyday.

There are some people who complain needlessly and endlessly about the lack of jobs or opportunities.

However, the reality is that life is full of opportunities. It just depends on what we are looking for, where we are looking, how we brace ourselves to fit into the myriad number of opportunities, and how we fight our paths forward to get those opportunities through determination and hard work.

There is no short cut in life, and certainly no short cut to success. You have got to earn it.

Human resource management and social media

I remember in the great economic depression of the 1980s, after I served in the army for national service, I was a school dropout with no college to go to, and hungry looking for a job.

Today, the recruitment scene is decidedly different. For one, I hardly see job applications in the mail as much, or at all. I remembered those days in the eighties, I was painstakingly looking through the recruitment pages of the newspapers every day, typing on the manual typewriters, and mailing out those applications in neatly written envelopes and postage stamps. Out of the thousands of applications I might have sent, I would get a few callbacks, and a few interviews.

Eventually, I was blessed to get a job with a quasi–government industrial laboratory testing organization as a junior laboratory assistant. Although I was only paid around US$200+ a month, I was elated I got a job.

Fast forward to today, and we see a complete transformation of how people would look for jobs. Using nothing but a few mouse clicks, an applicant can select jobs, attach his formatted curriculum vitae (CV), upload it with his credentials and photograph, and then wait for shortlisting to come through email or the phone.

If one happens to be looking for a job overseas, potential employers can even interview the applicant through videoconferencing. Social media, for one, is another vehicle for employers and employees alike, to connect.

For example, I have seen people looking for job opportunities on social media platforms such as LinkedIn and Facebook. Likewise, I have seen employers advertising job opportunities on the same platforms.

I am unsure if such platforms have already eroded the territories of traditional mainstream print media or job portals yet, but at least social media platforms are likely to expand job connectivity.

Companies advertise job vacancies, just as candidates advertise their desire for particular jobs, on social media platforms. It is also important to recognize what social media's impact is, and especially how that relate to a changing socio–psychological landscape of the emerging generation today.

In our days, we were rather private with our lives, and would prefer to only share those details with our families and close friends. Today, it is common to see younger people share every aspect of their lives, in text, in images, in motion video, etc. They would openly broadcast their joys and woes alike to the public through social media and their personal blogs.

My peers and I in human capital areas have noticed that while we sieve through applicants, we may need to be extra vigilant in discerning the suitability of such candidates today.

Just decades ago, we would examine job applications and shortlist a few, interview and profile them, discuss with management, and then after a couple more interviews, hire a person.

Today, we would receive job applications through email by the hundreds or thousands (depending on type of job), sieve through the applications, shortlist a few, and then, before we interview the applicants, go online to start our investigation. What do we look for?

For example, by looking for the public profiles of these applicants, we may understand their social behavior towards others. We may understand their likes and dislikes, their aspirations, their dreams (however divorced from our own corporate needs), and so on. Are these candidates straightforward or not? Are they social or antisocial? Are they too sociable to the extent of neglecting mainstream life? Are they exhibiting potentially dangerous or disturbing behavior that would impede their work in a collaborative work environment, or even society at large? Do they simply spend too much time, sometimes every other minute, on social media, that would be disastrous to their productivity? These and many more questions, and answers, can be discerned just by studying public broadcasts of some people.

Of course, these are not definitive answers, but they can raise valid questions that would demand solid answers before going forward.

Conversely, if a candidate has no social media presence or no public presence or content, that may raise some other questions as well.

Applying for a job today is simpler and faster for the emerging generation, in so far as technology empowerment goes. One no longer needs to travel to every destination by public transport, sweat the weather, and get doors literally slammed in one's face these days.

However, it certainly means a great deal more work for recruiters and human resource managers, to figure out a much more complex socio–psychological landscape, on top of trying to handle the same work as before, in a much more compressed timeframe.

The true winners are those candidates who are able to bridge and reduce the work for recruiters and HR managers, as well as their managers, deliver the results according to corporate goals, and genuinely smile and appreciate the job on their hands.

Employer–employee trust is a two–way street

When some of us who are human resource practitioners sit around and chat over coffee, one of the regular topics seem to be about trust.

It is easy to understand why employers and employees alike are talking about trust. The economic landscape today is volatile and uncertain. Is there a sustainable upturn? Is the economy, local, regional or global, truly on an upturn or just a temporary happy blip? With all the fanciful analytical tools we have, can we even have a fair assessment, much less a projection of the future?

Employees tend to believe it is important that they can trust their employers all the time. Employees expect their employers to be completely honest about the directions of the company, its financial health, if their jobs are secure, and so on. Unfortunately, in an increasingly volatile economic landscape, transparency, or trust, can be a rarity indeed.

Companies are laying off people just as quickly as people are recruited. "Permanent" contracts are fast becoming a relic, replaced by term contracts, or even independent contracts on a project basis.

There are two sides to this situation.

Employers are also facing the trust issue and bearing the heat. Many employers take great pains to go through laborious recruitment processes, to find who they perceive to be candidates suitable for shortlisting, go through all the difficult challenges of interviewing and background checks, and then more often than not, lose the good candidates very quickly to competitors or other industries. Thereafter, employers have to relive the unpleasant recruitment yet again, with costs (sometimes heavy) to bear.

Worse, recruited candidates are given training in the field and within the organizations, and before these recruits are proven sufficiently in the field or provide equitable returns for the company, the recruits leave for "better prospects." Again, the employer would have to restart the same recruitment process.

Therefore, trust is a two–way street.

What does an employer provide for an employee to earn that trust? Likewise, what does an employee provide in return for the laborious recruitment, the training and development, the opportunity to contribute and grow?

For employees, it would make sense to see things from the perspective of employers, and the labors the human resource and line managers go through. Employees can do more for the company to fight common battles on the same side, rather than draw battle lines against the very companies they work for. No employer wants to make unnecessary adversaries.

Don't list out what you learned, show me

Recently, we received many candidate submissions during a recruitment drive. One particular entry stood out.

His curriculum vitae had a long list of "Webinars" and seminars he attended, literally more than thirty.

Over the last two decades, I have enjoyed my journey as a keynote and conference speaker, as well as absorbing and learning as a conference attendee. Learning is a good thing, and continuing education is often a sign of a self–motivated individual. I applaud it.

The reality is that an attendee of a conference or a "Webinar" cannot conclusively prove what he has learned, simply because there is no exam at the end of the conference or "Webinar."

I read an article where a senior executive commented that experience is he values most in a candidate, no matter what certifications there may be, or may not be. I agree.

While we are talking about field experience, discerning what is actually written on a curriculum vitae is important.

For example, if a candidate came from a large department within a large organization, and stated that he is capable of managing or coordinating certain practices, projects or clients, it is inconclusive if indeed, such a candidate knows the entire workflow and process, or simply a portion of the entire process. In such a scenario, a candidate may merely be part of a large team that sees the process or project to successful completion, while the candidate only managed or worked on a small part of the process or project.

The best test of a candidate is not to listen or read the laundry list of achievements, certifications, or attendance to conferences or "Webinars." The best test is to have the candidate demonstrate his abilities during the interview.

For example, if a job requires copywriting, give the candidate a with a theme, a brief, and a mock exam on the spot to demonstrate his ability.

If you are looking for a social media or mobile app developer, have the candidate demonstrate to you his abilities with a simple campaign or prototype based on a generic theme, on his laptop, at your office. Sit with the candidate to see how he progresses through the prototyping process.

If the job requires preparing compelling slide presentations, give the candidate a mock theme for a client pitch or business meeting, and have the candidate sit in your office to complete the task – no bringing home "assignments" as you never know if the candidate completed the task, or someone else did.

Recruiting the best possible talents for today's environment is tough. There are many candidates out there, each with unique pitches. There are only a few openings, and increasingly less. The wisdom to discern how much practical, useful, and proven experience a candidate can bring to your table, is what counts.

Carpe diem, and not just your career

Even though we have very hot weather here, it is still invigorating to have a hot shower after a long work day.

One day, the water heater switch broke, and we needed an electrician to fix it. We found one and I took a morning off to wait for him. He turned out to be one of most interesting individuals I shared a conversation with, while he switched out the damaged switch for the new one. Let's call him Peter.

Peter asked me a strange question when he saw me, if my wife played the guitar and taught singing, pointing to the guitar in our living room. That was a really strange question.

Anyhow, I told Peter that my wife did not teach singing, but she wanted very much to learn how to play an instrument, and the guitar seems like a reasonable start.

Then Peter told me that he plays the Chinese string instrument "er hu" as well as cello!

I used to play the violin when I was young, and so I know how challenging the string instruments can be. We chatted quite a bit about Peter's musical interests, and I realized, despite his busy work running about different places fixing clients' electrical needs, he managed to learn the "er hu" and cello by himself, despite having no formal musical training and not knowing how to read music scores.

What I respect about Peter was that he was also able to use many classical Chinese lingo, something the modern generation has no clue about.

This is a truly learned man who learned many things by himself. In life, one can simply work to survive, or work with joy, and live with joy. Peter has shown that despite busy work, he will make an effort to learn to play not just one, but two musical instruments!

In anything that we do, do we find time to improve our work, and to learn things we have an interest in? Time is short and waits for no one, any minute lost will never be recovered again. Life, is what we make out of it.

Learning from a 85–year old master sushi chef

All too often, some of us who are leaders, face young people with haughty idealism. What can young people learn from the 85–year old Jiro Ono, master sushi chef?

I have seen my fair share of recruitment stories firsthand as a human capital practitioner, of junior to high–level positions, as well as recounted from peers during relaxing conversations over coffee.

One thing stands out from the current younger generation, compared to say, earlier generations.

In the eighties, when the great economic depression hit worldwide, many of us were just grateful to land a job of any kind. I have laboriously applied literally hundreds of roles, from trainee Teppanyaki chef, courier, administrative clerk, and so on, eventually landing a laboratory assistant job with a large industrial testing facility, at US$200+ a month. I had no complaints then, even if it meant I could only afford a bottle of milk for lunch. For me, and many of my peers and friends, we felt very blessed just to have a job, and the pay was secondary.

Fast forward to today, and the scenario is drastically different. I have seen candidates with a freshly minted degree, applying for entry–level jobs asking for US$2,400 or more a month, with no relevant or any experience whatsoever.

Yes, the cost of living has escalated drastically. But having no skills and experience does not make an excellent pitch for a high starting salary, especially if the candidate will merely be an apprentice where the team leaders have to dedicate precious time and effort to train this candidate for a long time, and sacrifice their own time that would have been productive hours.

When I teach a corporate program, I get paid by the client. Conversely, it would sound bizarre if a candidate demands a high starting salary while the employer trains the person, don't you think?

The acclaimed movie "Jiro Dreams of Sushi" was what rekindled this thought that compared many of us who fought through the great depression with a smile on our faces when we landed jobs without asking too much in return, and the current scenarios we face as seniors.

"Jiro Dreams of Sushi" is a documentary that talks about the 85–year old Jiro Ono–san, who runs (still) the Sukiyabashi Jiro, a small 10–seat sushi restaurant that has no other frills of cuisine except exquisite sushi lovingly and meticulously prepared through decades of commitment to excellence by Ono–san.

Young people who joined the small restaurant has to go through 10 years of difficult training before they can be confirmed as employees. Some would drop out, but those who braved the 10–year training will earn the stripes of recognition from everyone, as apprentices of the 85–year old master chef.

How many of us are willing to perfect our craft, continue to learn at all costs, to sacrifice time and effort to master the life goals we seek?

Ono–san has shown us it is possible, if one has heart. His apprentices have also shown that Ono–san is not an anomaly, but an elder who led the way for others to follow, and there are brave ones who have the heart and the humility to follow.

The meek shall inherit the earth. Many of us would gladly seek those with the true heart of an apprentice, and not those who merely seek silver dollars on the quick. After all, as many of us dig our heels in to fend off the ravaging economic storms, we need to then seek deeper to uncover the talented and worthy gems that can still be found, albeit taking much more effort.

Abrasive energy or benign diplomacy?

Some people are go–getters, and aren't afraid to ruffle some feathers to get things done, and sometimes, just to get things done at all costs.

So then, if you are looking for a candidate at your department or company, would you prefer a candidate with raw energy, or someone with tactfulness and grace?

I remember, regrettably, I used to be a go–getter and cared only for the end–results. Naturally, I didn't make many friends. One could argue that if you are immersed in a competitive financial services environment, you may not have time to even pause to think about anything else but completing tasks and achieving corporate objectives.

There are other people who are tactful and emotionally sensitive, where being able to get along with others may just be more important than simply achieving results.

I have known quite a few people who could really help soothe frayed nerves, even if sometimes, the competitive types might find these peaceful and sociable types not exactly moving at the same pace.

What kind of environment are you working in? Is your environment more suitable for competitive go–getters, or more for people who are team–players?

Yet, sometimes you can have your cake and eat it. There are the rare few, who combine positive energy with benign and even compassionate diplomacy. These are people you would like to hire at all costs, because they are natural leaders who are steadfast on deliverables and quality, and yet be empathetic to the needs of others with the grace of a diplomat, with energy that glows and shines on others.

Therefore, it is important to properly profile and study, communicate with, and especially listen well to candidates you are considering for jobs. Discern well, and you may just find the rare few people you would hire right on the spot.

A job is not all fun and glamor

Some young job candidates came forward to demand many things: Pay, perks, short hours, well–furnished office, and most of all, that the jobs should be what they want, how they want it, mostly full of fun, social engagement, and glamor.

Unfortunately, we don't live in a fictional world of movies and make–believe.

When we recruit new people, we seldom oversell the job itself. We would always tell them, for any and every job, there may be 20% of the job that we have great interest for. The remaining 80% would likely be mundane, backend, support, or administrative in nature. There is no job in the world that is 100% glamor and fun, or easy.

For example, even a Hollywood actor may only see 20% or less of fun and glamor (appearing before adoring fans and maybe, just maybe, winning a prestigious film award). The rest of the time is fighting to get roles in countless castings (and often not getting the gigs), reading screen plays, rehearsing ad nauseam every line in the script, NG, NG and NG during shooting, etc, etc.

So people need to learn to respect the job they have and know that as long as 20% of the job is interesting, challenging, stimulating and fun, the 80% is necessary.

See that kind young man helping someone? Recruit him!

What do you think is the single most important attribute I would look for in an employee, contractor, or partner? No, it is not ambition, or even talent. It is something much closer to my heart.

Just a short while ago, we drove to the office to park, and passed by two people whose interaction made a strong impression on us.

We have already seen in some reports how emotionless some young people can be, and how apathy and a lack of expression somehow have surfaced increasingly.

The rise of consumerism and materialism, coupled with individualism and ambition, seem to have created a "subculture" of some people lacking sympathy for others.

We drove by a young man, who walked past an old physically challenged old man in a wheelchair, and then he walked back and patiently and carefully helped the old wheelchair–bound man across the street. That scene made a moving impression.

That was also when I realized, from many of the interviews and testing of candidates we have come across, either for our own needs and for clients, one of the attributes that always stood out above all else, was empathy.

If a person is a self–starter, a fast and eager learner, and is meticulous and careful in his work, these are all desirable attributes in an employee, a contractor, or a business partner. However, when a person rises above the fray and shows empathy for others, that is when all other qualities pale in comparison, and such a person wins my heart rather than just a checklist.

To me at least, a person with empathy is willing to go the extra mile for the needs of others, especially those with less. Such a person is willing to do things for a humane reason, more than he is paid for, and needs no rallying to serve the higher needs of others and the community. Often, such a person may not crave for unnecessary power and wealth just to "get ahead". This person is willing to go the extra mile, therefore tend to put in more effort to learn, to adapt, to perform, and above all, do things ethically without the need for constant supervision.

These are rare gems, and harder to come by these days. When you identify someone with empathy as the tip of his attribute iceberg, dig deeper, and you may just find this person the person you have been looking for your organization for a long time.

Publish or perish – the new world of careers and business

What kind of public presence does a person have, may very well determine just how much sought after this person may be in the near term and beyond. The landscape of job and opportunity hunting is rapidly changing.

Dan Schawbel wrote a thought–provoking piece*, on why a person's online presence will replace the resume in a decade. In my opinion, the escalation of the social media phenomenon means that this projection might happen much sooner, if not already.

When we seek out potential candidates for our work, or on behalf of clients, one of the things we always look beyond is the resume of those candidates. We tend to seek out their social media presence, and discern what kind of personality and attributes such a person might have, obvious or otherwise.

There will be some candidates with little social media presence or none at all, and those will tend to be more difficult to discern, especially for roles that would involve communication in a social context, since there will already be a large pool of potential candidates to look at given a time constraint.

And from others, we can determine what kind of social presence, what kind of contextual knowledge, what kind of personal interest, what kind of social interaction skills, how genuine and personal the social interaction, and so on. These and many other areas are how many practitioners discern what kind of potential candidates we are looking at. After all that

74

preliminary work, there may be profiling, practical tests, and background checks, before a shortlist of candidates is found.

So for jobseekers who desire to build a long–term career, it is important, especially today, to begin to build up a social media presence that is not merely a report of personal and social meetings, but perhaps expand and extend one's knowledge, slowly and steadily, as one progresses through studies and work. In a world where more opportunities are contract–based and even "intrapreneurial," there is a need to show independent, clear, intelligent, mellow, and expansive thinking through published works. It won't be easy – it takes patience, consistency, tenacity, all attributes also desired in candidates.

When I finished my doctoral programs in business and later theology, one of the constant thoughts that resonated in my head was what many academics told me often, "publish or perish." I took that admonition seriously.

In business, it is the same thing. It is no longer sufficient to hide a body of knowledge to ourselves and only use it when engaged. Prospects and clients might need to see a public display of content and knowledge, and even wisdom, that we as practitioners profess to have.

So, as business and communication leaders, we too, must continue to publish often, through any useful social media or Web platform, that can be propagated to as many people as we can, to share our knowledge, to alert others of potential pitfalls in running a business, to build on what all of us know so expand our knowledge in quantum leaps.

Thoughts are only fleeting ideas, unless we solidify them on a concrete platform, whether it be ink and paper, or digital bits that are stored on a storage medium. Such ideas even when solidified, become only truly compelling and useful when we share them, discuss them, and then refine them into something truly executable, repeatable, and useful to others.

http://www.forbes.com/sites/danschawbel/
2011/02/21/5–reasons–why–your–online–
presence–will–replace–your–resume–in–10–years/

Toxic employees under the microscope

While businesses and owner–managers are fighting tooth and nail in an increasingly difficult economy (and worsening), they would need to put everything under the microscope to see how best to move their businesses forward, even if painfully.

Let's face it, we are facing difficult times ahead. The economy is no longer a simple microscopic depression, but one that baffles even governments, states, and even regional economies. Every peg in the machinery of a business, becomes critical to moving the entire business forward. Even one weak or dysfunctional peg, can slow a business down to oblivion and destruction.

I was reading an interesting article by Ms Janine Popick, CEO of Vertical Response, in INC. Magazine's website, (one of the best business magazines I would recommend), on what she defined as "poison employees."*

She briefly described 3 types of employees that would drag a business down, (1) those who whine, (2) those who gossip, and (3), those who hide.

I concur with Ms Popick's incisive insights. As a fellow owner–manager and a human resource development (HRD) practitioner, let me elaborate and add some others.

1. There are **those who complain** all the time. Some of these employees simply complain as a means to let off steam, which can be understandable. Some others may have more deep–rooted problems that may, or may not be able to be

resolved through counseling and discussion. Those who mean to simply let off steam, however, may invariably jeopardize others in their work environment and reduce overall team morale, which then becomes a bad thing. With the onslaught of social media and blogging, some employees may even let off steam online, not realizing the potentially viral power of their messages online, and invariably cause damage to the reputation of the businesses they work for, and their own personal reputation. After all, it is difficult to erase published messages online, and those may come back to haunt the very people who innocently (or otherwise) posted complaints online. Some may even become bigger legal issues to contend with. Is it worth the rant for employees who more often than not, simply want a steadily growing career path in life? For businesses, if an open communication is maintained with employees, then owner–managers should make clear to employees that all issues should be resolved directly, and malice, however innocent, is not something to be taken lightly, since complaints will always bite both ways and have greater repercussions that one may realize.

2. **Those who gossip** can be a real legal time bomb. Many businesses would have employees or associates sign nondisclosure agreements (NDAs) which are very specific in information and distribution. However, some employees are naturally gossipy and may invariably mention confidential information to friends and families, and cause such information to leaked to the media, or other people who should have no privy to such information. While those who gossip may consider it harmless, the harm is much greater than they can imagine, and may have serious legal and

financial implications for the stakeholders, including lawsuits, criminal cases, and big financial payouts. Therefore, businesses must educate all employees and associates on the importance of nondisclosure, and what are the implications for information leakage, and that those who choose to gossip, will be summarily dealt with, no exceptions.

3. **Those who hide away** can become a real drag to team and business productivity, because the rest of the team mates would have to carry the bulk of the work. Many businesses see an increase in becoming "microcosmized" (what I consider a decentralizing of decision–making and task completion), there is less segmentation of tasks, and everyone in the small teams have to do a lot more in a distributed work environment. When someone lazes around, the rest of the team will feel the pressure immediately. Therefore, for supervisors and leaders, such behavior cannot be condoned and must be counseled, and subsequent action be swift and decisive so that everyone knows the importance of working together in teams and cooperating well with one another. Leaders should set clear goals and targets, and measure each person based on how much self–empowerment and self–learning an employee takes on. Those who are told to do just one thing, but takes the initiative to learn another, and then offer to help out to do another task, should be recognized and rewarded more than those who simply moves an inch when you tell them to move an inch. No one who is drawing pay is exempt from work, and those who do not work, deserve no pay and no employment.

4. There are some **who are too calculative**. Many HR recruiters have seen young upstarts who would demand much more

pay and benefits than they qualify for, or are proven for. I have also seen some people demanding that they would only do particular tasks, and would not want to put in extra effort for the collective team efforts, whether in additional work hours or tasks. The trouble is that such people create a negative atmosphere at work, invariably causing others in the team to feel that perhaps they should not bother to help each other too. Therefore, such calculative people should be isolated and rooted out, and allow the team to see that collaborative efforts and an open mind and heart are desired attributes. It is truly a collective effort these days, and that all of us are like team mates on a football game, or rowers in a dragon boat competition. We move in the same direction, using all of our might and minds, together.

5. There are **some who are prima donnas**. Prima donnas are great in singular environments where they are supposed to shine to their utmost. For example, if you are a solo singer, you are to be brilliant, because you would do everyone justice simply by being your best. In a typical environment, even the most brilliant minds and the most talented hands, have to play well together in a team, and not step over or crush others in a team for one's own glory. Prima donnas who roughshod others in a work place, are to be pulled aside and counseled and rebuked, and reminded that team work is valued above all else. If such prima donnas continue to roughshod others, it is wiser for a leader to let go such an employee rather than to create resentment and dissent among the rest of the team. No one is an island at the work place, and even the best need others to bring forth brilliance.

There is no better time, than the roughest of moments as we ride the depressing economic times ahead, than to be a positive and contributing part of a greater team, to cheer our team mates on together, to fight together, to learn new things together, to grow together, to survive together, and to thrive together. May the best team win.

http://www.inc.com/janine–popick/3–types–of–poison–employees.html

dot zen 2.0

Customer Service & Sales

Wisdom of parting ways with customers

When thinking of business and revenue growth, sometimes we may lose sight of the long haul and focus only on short–term gains. When and what should prompt us to move on to greener pastures?

The simplest idea to grow a business and its revenue, seems to be gaining as many customers as possible.

For large companies with great infrastructure, financial muscle, and armies of employees, that seems like not too difficult a task to handle.

However, for emerging or smaller companies, keeping pace with simply acquiring more customers, is a fine art that requires discernment and wisdom. There are many small innovative companies, in my opinion, that have made a difference.

I am an amateur photographer and filmmaker, and I follow photographic and video–graphic developments very closely. I try to research what would work for me, especially with my physical constraints (myopia and scoliosis). For me, I need cameras that work for stills, as well as high–definition (HD) video. Some equipment may work better for me than others.

For example, while many would swear by professional cameras such as Leica, alas, these cameras typically do not have image stabilization and some may even require manual focus, both of which pose great challenges to someone with poor eyesight. Further, many of these professional still cameras are not designed as HD video cameras primarily. However, I have found the Olympus OM–D EM5, which uses a smaller micro four–third (MFT) sensor, having an advanced image stabilization and very responsive autofocus, to work for me wonderfully to capture moments that are very fleeting.

Don't get me wrong. I love the Leica for what it stands for and what it can do for the serious users. However, in a fast–paced multimedia environment and for someone like me, I need a different tool. The OM–D, the Panasonic Lumix GH2 and GH3, all work for me as still photography

tools, as well as for amateur videography on the cheap, with accessibility to external sound inputs, HD video capture, and interchangeable lenses from various makers (including the esoteric Voigtländer fast primes, such as the 17.5mm f/0.95 which I love with the follow focus).

Whether a tool is "more" branded or more expensive, does not matter to me. The tool should work for me and serve my needs. Therefore, when smaller companies innovate, such as the Asia–based SLR Magic with its innovative fast prime lenses for various mounts, including

the MFT mount, there will be people who can benefit from and appreciate such innovations.

Conversely, there will be detractors. So although SLR Magic will no longer develop rangefinder coupled lenses, they will focus on developing more lenses for videographers like us, which have click–less apertures and even geared focus rings for our follow focus units. The SLR Magic lenses can work with my Olympus OM–D, GH2, GH3, and other MFT cameras, as well as the latest Blackmagic Cinema Camera with MFT mount, which is a digital filmmaker's dream tool. So, an innovative small company like SLR Magic will continue to attract specific customers with tools that serve them.

So what has SLR Magic got to do with parting ways with customers?

Analogously, in many industries, sometimes we are faced with the dilemma of having a customer whose account does not add up, based on profitability or whether we feel appreciated or not. Do we continue to brave through the challenges with little or no reward, financial or emotive, or do we part ways?

The answer is simpler than we make it out to be. All too often, what do we seek in life? Happiness. There will be people who we enjoy working with, and people we don't. There will be things we like, and things we don't. If the dollars are not worth the effort and the pains, why continue to frustrate ourselves?

After all, health and happiness are some of the most important things to many people. When we free up the time and resources by parting ways with an account that we are thoroughly demoralized by, we would lose some dollars which might have paid some bills and some staffers, but the emotive pressures would be alleviated and we have our minds and hearts liberated to seek greener pastures. And there will always be other pastures to graze.

Sure, it is going to be challenging finding new business, but when there is a will, there is a way, and there is always someone out there who would appreciate our talents and experience better, and the working and collaboration styles more collegial.

Remember too, not all detractors are even paying customers, and may never ever be. For businesses with limited resources (big and small alike), we have to have the discernment and the wisdom to know which battles to fight.

We must try to remember that in life, there will always be those who cheer us on and are with us, and there will be those who jeer and oppose us. We can't live our lives swayed merely by the opinions of a few. Life is barely a short glimpse in time and may be fleeting. It is worth every second of our lives to make it worth our time, resources, and hearts.

4 tips to prevent sales and service black holes

The best customer service is often found when you are not a big customer, when the obvious financial returns to the salesperson seems to be small and uncertain.

Have you ever felt as if you are getting sucked into a black hole when talking to some salespeople?

I am often dressed in very old t–shirts and faded pants when I not teaching or speaking, especially if I am simply working behind my desk.

Whenever I go to the nearby hawker center or some food courts, I usually get great service from the stalls I frequent despite how dressed down I may be, with friendly service and sometimes even get more food than I ordered. I am touched by their gestures, and of course, I would gladly return often.

Sometime ago, we started to re–embrace some of our earlier offerings, that of video news releases (VNRs) to clients, and to set up micro–sites meant for communicating client news content in a more audiovisual manner.

More people hear and see news and content through video channels, rather than flipping through pages or even reading lines and lines of text online. While we are familiar with on–demand video production from videography and filmmaking, the realm of "live" video streaming is something we were not previously familiar with. Therefore, we started to study the available technologies and dived right into various technologies

— the fastest way to learn in a short time. There are many options available in the "live" video streaming area, from proprietary streaming providers (there are a handful of very big companies), to content delivery networks (CDNs), which we are already familiar with when developing and delivering content through Web channels.

Out of the proprietary streaming providers, I first tried a handful of them, but the video quality for "live" streaming was not up to my expectations versus the price I had to pay.

Then I approached another proprietary streaming provider, and I received a cheerful email reply from a junior sales associate. I relayed to her my needs and hoped for a good package for a small firm like ours. I received her reply promptly, but the content of the email disappointed me. I was given the standard retail rate, which was too expensive for the functionality it provides.

Thankfully, I was able to locate two other streaming providers, one of which was a very established one, DaCast, and another, upLynk.

With upLynk, the service provides the customer with a simplified uploading process, and an intelligent encoding process that took much of the work from the customer. It is a promising service and I will very likely sign up, not just because the functionality is good for small firms  like us, but the CMO Ken Brueck wrote personally to me to say that they are happy to work with small firms, and gave me some very reassuring technical advice.

 With DaCast, the service works with real–time messaging protocol (RTMP) streaming, which I needed with my wireless encoder and transmitter, and just like upLynk, offers affordable pricing that small firms like us can use. The quality of DaCast's "live" streaming is great, the site offers specific technical configuration for my equipment, and I got very good service from their technical support team as well, despite knowing I am just a tiny customer.

When we signed up with OpenDNS (opendns.com) to help us stem out malware and provide safe Internet browsing for our team, the company was empathetic to our size, and was able to also work out a preferential package tailored just for us.

Nothing is impossible – all it takes is a listening ear and go–to action.

Right now, we can readily offer our clients the entire workflow to shoot HD footage for "live" news events and launches, as well as encoding them for on–demand viewing later, all wrapped together in custom micro–sites.

Small companies may be small by choice or design, or may simply be just emerging with plenty of room to grow. Any personalized customer and technical support you can provide to a small company will be imprinted in their minds and endear you as a partner. It is not just about the obvious financial returns, but the goodwill that you bring to the table that will carry your brand and your products and services farther and wider than you imagine, because these business owners will invariably sing praises about you to many others. Think far and wide, and endear yourself with your prospects with personalized and empathetic service, however small they may appear to be.

For service providers, when talking to a prospective customer, here are some important things to remember:

1. Be **attentive and empathetic** to the needs of the customer, and find internal expertise to address technical and esoteric requirements the customer needs.

2. Remember that smaller companies often have no internal expertise and would rely on you, the service provider, to provide some **pointers and expertise** before the purchase.

3. **Follow up promptly, and follow through** the sales process to conclusion, whether the prospective customer becomes a paying customer or not.

4. Work out **preferential packages and rates** that cater to the exacting needs of smaller and emerging companies. Talk to your senior management if possible.

Companies are looking for stars, whether they are salespeople or customer support specialists. Companies are not looking for people who simply behave like black holes.

The conundrum of "the customer is always right"

Decades ago, when I was entrenched in total quality management (TQM) and service quality, everyone seemed to be hypnotized by the idea that the customer is always right. The war cry then, especially by line managers, was to bark down at front–liners to deliver service with the motto of "the customer is always right."

Fast forward to the twenty–first century, and many things have changed. Technology has empowered just about anybody to find information quickly, and to reach out to people real–time. Anyone can connect to another by the click of the mouse or a swipe on the tablet or smartphone. Anyone can exchange ideas or communicate feelings through social media or mobile apps.

So, is the customer always right? Was the idea "the customer is always right" even "right" to begin with? Ponder with me.

The customer is not just the external paying customer who pays a service or product provider. Your internal employees who serve external paying customers or other internal colleagues are also customers, non–paying customers to be exact. In fact, you may be paying them. The customer is also an external shareholder, who believes in your company enough to buy shares of your company (if your company is listed on the stock exchange). The customer may also be external stakeholders such as non–profits and beneficiaries of your corporate social responsibility programs, or even the journalists from the media who hear from you now and then.

In short, the customer is not just external paying customers, but just about anyone we have a commercial or social exchange with at work.

Therefore, if we restrict the notion "the customer is always right" only to external paying customers, what about our employees who are valuable people who create value by serving paying customers and internal employees alike? They too, are customers. What about the journalists and broadcast producers? They are valuable customers who we need to engage consistently and truthfully, so that our corporate brand continues to fly high. Likewise, our shareholders are valuable customers too. Their faith in our company will ensure its continued survival for the long haul.

Imagine if we insist only external paying customers are "always right," our employees will fight low morale all the time and staff turnover will be raging, and our processes will falter and fail. But if we insist our employees are "always right," then our paying customers, external stakeholders such as the media and shareholders, may be antagonized. You get the picture.

It is akin to a marriage. If a wife insists on being right all the time, the husband will walk out of the marriage. And if a husband insists he is right all the time, his wife will insist on a divorce soon.

How then, can we embrace customer service in an enlightened manner? The simplest way to look at it is to approach the idea of marriage again.

Is a husband always right? No. Is a wife always right? No. Is insisting who is right all the time the key issue to a successful marriage? Certainly not! Then, what is?

The key issue is mutual respect. When a husband respects the opinions and actions of his wife, and his wife does the same for him, a sustainable marriage becomes a greater possibility.

Think of customer service as akin to a beautiful waltz or tango between a married couple. When one of them moves forward, the other steps back, and vice versa. It is poetry in action.

Likewise, it is never important to insist who is right in customer service. The paying customer is never "always right." The internal employees or external stakeholders are never "always right." The key issue is to have a culture of mutual respect between all parties. The company respects the external suppliers to pay bills on time when receiving goods and services. The internal employees respect colleagues, paying customers and external stakeholders. Likewise, the external paying customers are accorded the same corporate culture so that they will provide the same mutual respect for the internal teams. It is gentry respecting the gentry.

In this closed loop of enlightened service, mutual respect for all parties is the guiding light, and not an insistence of who is right. Trash the notion that "the customer is always right." Instead, inculcate a culture of mutual respect where external paying customers, external stakeholders (shareholders, media and suppliers), internal customers, are all given fair and equal respect. This is the enlightened service that is sustainable.

After all, Mencius (372–289 BCE), student of Confucius, believed that humans are different from animals, and possess benevolence for others.

Mencius said that if a child falls, it is the inner nature of a human to feel sympathetic towards the child. Therefore, unless external and internal factors prevent a person from being respectful to another, it is the tendency of a person to be respectful to others.

Respect begets respect, and this is the highest form of customer service.

3 tips of managing retail staff

Have you been to a shop where the retail assistants would tail you around the shop, so much so that you end up walking out of the shop fast?

Retail is tough business. My family has been in retail and distribution for a long time. I can tell you it is not a business for the faint–hearted, and certainly not a business for those who are clueless about serving people well.

Customer service is perhaps as old as human history, when people started bartering things of value with each other. The process of negotiation can take many forms, and given that humans are emotive creatures, the best transactions come from happy conversations and good feelings.

Much of customer service today is still the same, albeit refined many quantum leaps ahead. Fundamentally, customer service is still about mutual respect between suppliers and customers, so much so that an exchange or transaction will take place smoothly, and a relationship can be nurtured and developed into a long–term one.

Every visit I remembered of Japan, has been one of service excellence. Whether I was visiting a large departmental store, an electronics supermarket, a restaurant, a hotel, a small ramen shop at the roadside, or hopping into a cab, I was never greeted with disdain or suspicion, but with courtesy and respect.

I am a "gaijin" (foreigner) who speaks little Japanese, but the lack of convergence between my native languages and theirs, never once caused the Japanese folks I met to sprout a reluctance to provide great service. They would go through hoops to ensure I was properly served, either by dragging someone faraway who speaks a little English, to perhaps trying to use sign language and the written Japanese (which I can comprehend due to the Kanji characters).

In short, their service is never hampered even by language or cultural limitations.

Conversely, I am a frequent visitor to a local technology mall. The service at the average shop is not stellar, though not that dismal either. It is fortunate that I often take great pains to learn whatever I need to at my own time, so that when I do visit the mall, I am prepared and will already know what I need and want.

However, there is one shop that I consistently try to explore, but would eject myself out within seconds. The typical visit is that I would walk in, and a retail assistant would begin to ask the usual question "can I help you?" The trouble is, when someone asks such a question, they have to be prepared to back up that claim, and these retail assistants with little or no computing knowledge, often fails miserably at "helping" anyone, especially someone of a geek like me. Then the retail assistant would start tailing me just a breath away behind me, as I try to walk through their galleys. They have about 5 retail assistants all focusing their gaze on you (simply because this shop doesn't seem to attract any customer). You would then feel so uncomfortable you have to walk out of the shop so quickly as if you are in a dungeon of roaches. Then I would suddenly remember why I never bought anything from them before, at least until my aging memory somehow leads me to meander into the same shop maybe a year or two later.

Customer service is not easy to teach, especially if the cultural backdrop does not provide one where social etiquette, courtesy and mutual respect are nurtured. But manners can be learned, and knowledge of products and services can certainly be learned. It simply takes discipline, effort, hard work, and patience.

1. When employing front—line employees for retail, it is important to **profile them** so that they are suitable for successful human interaction. Not everyone is suited for interacting with others, and not everyone likes to converse. Some people are more suited for back—office roles. There is nothing wrong with that. We need to fit the right people with the right roles.

2. Make it a point to have front—line employees **learn well** the products and services you carry. It takes effort on your part as an employer, and it demands effort from employees too. If an employee has no interest to learn about the products and services you carry, why should such a person work at your shop, much less, get paid? It is after all, an equitable relationship whereby an employee puts in the prerequisite effort and hard work demanded for a job, and the employer pays this employee fairly and promptly. It is a simple relationship.

3. **Reward** those front—line employees who consistently provide great customer service, and who consistently improve upon their craft, their knowledge, and their interactions. Make it known to all the employees of what is demanded of them,

and why some are recognized through awards, better pay, or promotions. Not everyone is suited for a career in retail and distribution, and many will drop out. Reward those few who excel well. Their good nature and service, their work ethic, their continuous learning, will rub off on the new entrants who share the same dreams.

The economy continues to cloud the horizon. The challenges faced by the retail and distribution industry may therefore heighten. We need people who can brave the challenges with us, soldiering forward, with a genuine smile and good nature to carry through the storm.

Ills of short messages – did you really mean that?

Have you been on the receiving end of the ills of short messaging? Can short replies convey the nuances and the meaning of what we hope to communicate? Do we owe it to the recipients to explain ourselves in sufficient detail, even if it demands more from us?

Recently, a friend was looking around for a senior–level job, and I happen to chance upon a one–liner from a recruiter's post online. Out of a genuine desire to help my friend, I enquired about the job with the recruiter, asking very politely for some brief information. I am from the human resource field since the 1980s, and certainly appreciate just sufficient information to make sense, but certainly not information that would be privy only between the recruiter and the candidates.

When the recruiter replied, I was a little startled. He replied with:

"Absolutely not."

Now, perhaps instant and short messaging has gotten to many people today, with pressure getting on their otherwise good sensibilities. I understand that, but would have appreciated a different response from a fellow practitioner.

What could the response have been then? As a service quality consultant, I might have said something akin to:

"Thank you so much for thinking of our firm! It would be a privilege to serve your friend and our clients in cementing a good job match together. However, it would be difficult to share too much information with a third–party from our firm's practices. Would you be willing to share your friend's details and contacts with me instead? I am grateful for you helping us!"

Everyone faces work pressure these days – it is the nature of the fiercely competitive world we live in today. You have a challenging time at work. I would have an equally challenging time at work. The world is a small place and paths can cross, sometimes uncannily again, and again.

Like the Chinese folk saying goes, "Keep an open path for people to retreat to."

Therefore, make an effort to extend a reply to a request, even if it means a slight delay (not a long delay), that would help reduce doubt and concerns, provide sufficient information, and most of all, create a better engagement experience or a smile to the recipient. Everyone would welcome a better day ahead.

Sending sales pitches to competitors?

Have you received emails wanting to do business with you, unfortunately from a competing firm? It may sound redundant and even hilarious to some, but we do a little research about who we email to pitch our business.

I received an email starting with "dear valued customer...," which is common for email spam not addressed to a particular person, since we aren't customers – but no big deal.

Then the email got interesting. The sender started to mention that he saw our banner ad, and that he represented a social media marketing firm that helps companies get on Facebook, before launching into a block of cut–and–paste text of "blah–blah–blah" about how useful the medium is, and that they have "more than 25 million viral reach on..."

First, I checked out their website, and found that they are a direct competitor to our firm.

We are a holistic communications firm that provides tactical delivery with technology, public relations, human capital development, as well as social media. Their company is more of a social media outfit that claims to do public relations as well. We won't use their outfit for sure. A cursory browse–through on our website would have more than definitively allow a cold–caller to know what we do and offer (what we do is prominently shown as a tagline on our website), as well as who the principals are. A cursory check through the search engines would have also easily revealed what we do for a living.

Second, any professional social media outfit would not guarantee anything, much less make grander claims about social media than they can really deliver. The social media population is certainly growing in an exponential pace, but without understanding what a client's business is and how best to target the RIGHT audience with the RIGHT marketing tools, there is absolutely no way you can guarantee anything.

There may be millions of social media users out there, but the actual consumer population within any country that uses social media to buy products may be a very small number compared to those who frequent physical stores. Social media is but one of the marketing tools in a complete arsenal available to holistic marketers, and no marketer worth his salt will recommend only one single marketing tool and claim to guarantee sensational results.

When we want to pitch a prospect cold, the minimum we would do is to go to their website and figure out what the prospect does. Search engines are not difficult to use, and there can be tons of data readily available.

If there is no data at all available on the Internet, perhaps then the next step is to find out from trade directories what the prospect does, before attempting to cold call or email (if available) the prospect.

Don't pitch blind, don't pitch without research, and certainly, don't pitch your competitors. It is euphemistically speaking, ignorant.

Right fit for retail sales?

Working in a retail outlet is never easy, especially in the harsh economic climate we experience today. Yet, having an exemplary service attitude is mandatory for both the survival of the retail outlet, and the career of the retail salesperson.

During the same day, I experienced two extremes of retail service.

I was at a large electronics supermarket to shop for a new fridge as the current one is near its end. When I walked towards a fridge I wanted to check out, a tall slim young man approached and pestered me with the usual spiel, "Can I help you?" Of course, I declined and told him I did not need his help. I started examining the various technical specifications (including physical dimensions to fit into my narrow space), and shortlisted two models. The same salesperson kept coming back to introduce another brand's model, and insisted that I should choose that instead. That particular model simply did not fit my needs, and he started pushing other models of the same brand, leading me to believe he wasn't keen to serve my needs as a customer, but rather, his own commission.

After that, I needed to look for ingredients for dinner, and checked out a small new shop selling pasta and spaghetti. A young man came to serve us and was polite, knowledgeable, and sensitive to our needs. We bought some pasta. We returned later another day to buy even more pasta to give to family members.

Some people insist that salespeople can be "trained." You can teach good salespeople the necessary product and technical knowledge so that they can serve customers better, but you really can't "train" someone to be salespeople. What does that mean?

The right salespeople are those who are sensitive to people and their needs. They are communicative, sociable, warm and friendly. They are earnest and eager to learn, and hardworking. Above all, they realize that only truly serving the needs of others result in the success of their own careers. The truly great salespeople are people with the right personality mix with the above attributes. You can't "train" someone to be warm – at most, you can merely "train" someone to "appear" warm. You can't "train" someone to be sociable either. A person is sociable to begin with, or he is not.

Likewise, you can't force someone to learn. A person should want to and desire to learn on his own. No amount of incentivizing can transform a laggard into a performer.

Over the course of my human resource development journey, I realized that you can't do much for people who don't value their jobs and who merely want to pass time.

In short, sieve out the personalities and character attributes that are already present in an individual, and groom such an individual with opportunities for learning, serving others, and this individual will shine.

Don't try to recruit people simply by a submitted curriculum vitae, or to meet "headcount". Recruit the right type of individuals for the right jobs. Reward the brilliant individuals appropriately, and transfer away those who simply can't fit in.

You are accountable for the success or failure of the company, as well as the livelihood for all the employees. Different people fit into different jobs, and not everyone is meant to do sales, just as not everyone is meant to be chief executives or office administrators.

In the fierce retail sales front, every customer encounter counts – especially at the cash register.

Pressure or partnership with your suppliers?

All too often, we hear of companies pressuring their suppliers and partners to perform. However, as we are all humans, what would work better?

Human dignity is important, and mutual respect is often the hallmark of successful business relationships. While some companies and even management thinkers have pushed for ideas such as "key performance indicators" (KPIs), we have progressively seen how such ideas and measurements often work against them in the long run.

In recent history, the collapse and restructuring of various industries, including the once untouchable financial industry, is a timely and grim reminder that behind pressuring for performance, comes a heavy penalty.

Look way back at successful companies, and you can easily find a different mindset altogether – sustainability.

Look around the world, whether the West, or the East, which is fast becoming the cornerstone of success, there are large and small companies that are not only successful, but have been sustainable over a long time. These companies are not shooting stars of brilliant but transient prominence, but the result of a very slow, steady and painful ascension to what they are today.

What are some of the reasons of these sustainable successes, especially in Asia? At least two things – (1) Sheer hard work with no shortcuts, and (2) mutual respect for others.

Business relationships are built slowly and steadily in my culture. People are at the very least courteous, and respect is the key to forging sustainable and favorable business relationships. This is perhaps a hint of the Confucian lineage we subconsciously live by. Unlike the notion that one can create a "hot" product or service and make a quick profitable exit, hard work instead, is the hallmark of slowly and steadily inching towards something you can call your own. The "dot–com" idea is not what we subscribe to, and we don't believe there is a quick road to success. At most, it is a quick flash.

Therefore, in the same light of hard work and mutual respect, how should we see our suppliers? Do we simply imagine that pushing them ever towards performance and results will be to our benefit? Are our imagined goals even realizable or realistic, or just figures we pluck out of thin air? Does pressure create any sense of partnership with our suppliers?

Conversely, a true partnership is a sharing of journeys, a convergence of goals, and at the end of the day, an enjoyable path together. You cannot call a business relationship a "partnership" if you insist only upon the performance of your suppliers, without putting an equitable amount of commitment into the relationship to secure your supplier's success and performance.

So if you are selling products, you would need a sizable marketing campaign to help your retailers perform up to your sales targets. If you are working with suppliers requesting products or services quickly, you are expected to pay your suppliers promptly on time as well. If you expect sizable media coverage from your brands, you would have to commit sizable dollars to not just fees, but advertising dollars and campaigns that can truthfully create an impression that you are as big as you claim you are.

Respect begets respect, and your partners will feel like true partners, and not imagine themselves to be slaves without recognition. Likewise, true respect is about understanding the realities of the world, the challenges your partners face, and how to collectively and collegially cooperate to reach beneficial goals.

You might be pleasantly surprised how easy it is for your partners to perform well, not under duress, but under mutual respect.

Pressure is something you do to cook a dish (in a pressure cooker). Leave it there, and nowhere near a human relationship. Life is not just about numbers. Life is about living, with people, and having a smile to go to bed with.

Wisdom of the open space gatherings of village elders

Have you stepped into a store and found sales assistants tagging behind you asking "can I help you" and not allowing you to shop in peace? Or have you gone online and have people stalking you and hoping there will be a business relationship?

Harassing someone to close a deal or to create a business relationship is just not smart business. It is the surefire way to lose a potential deal, annoy a prospect, and chase away people. There are many schools of thought, sometimes in conflict with one another, on what good sales techniques are.

Allow me to present some insights based on field experience. In a shop, if I am a sales assistant, I would give a little time for visitors to first get comfortable and immersed into my shop. Genuinely happy to see the visitors, I would then introduce myself:

"Hi, I am ABC, and I am a sales assistant with XYZ Shop. Please take your time to browse and try out the products in the shop. If you need me at any time, whether to explain the product features, or promotions, I will be at this corner. Thank you so much for visiting us!"

Then, allow the visitors to take their time. Be respectful of their personal space, and their desires to browse, to try the products on display, or when they are keen, to chat with us. By then, they are interested prospects. What about online? The art of social networking is simple. Would you dare harass someone in real life and stalk them around? Strict laws aside, it is just bad manners. Nobody likes to associate with someone who harasses or bullies another. Rather, everyone desires a friend.

This brings to mind the very cool and ancient art of the indigenous peoples of the Americas. In those days, when there was a problem to be resolved, the tribe would gather round a fire, and there would be a facilitator. Nobody would disrespect another in this problem—solving scenario, and every person who had something to contribute, would air his views. At the end, the facilitator, who did not assert control, would gather all views, and found the best possible way to resolve the problem together. All those who gathered round the fire would abide by the decision of the group, and trusted the outcomes – no matter what the outcomes may be.

How the indigenous peoples of the Americas did it so long time ago, can also be found in conciliatory and collaborative work environments in corporations today, and certainly can be applied to customer service and business networking scenarios easily as well.

The next time your people are found breathing down the necks of potential customers and business associates, pull them back, and give everyone some space. Everyone likes space and the freedom. With a relaxed mind, you may forge friendships, which are more valuable than just a single business deal. The world, after all, is small these days.

Fanciful formatting blocking your sales and interactions?

Email communication is the staple of modern marketing and communication, having supplanted at least partially, more traditional ways to communicate with prospects and customers. Email works very differently from a telephone call, allowing the sender to send tailored messages to many people at the same time, compared to a telephone call which demands the full attention of you communicating with another person.

Many of us receive sales or marketing–related emails from businesses, the media, research companies, non–profits, and even government agencies.

How often have you received emails that showed you this?

"Sorry, you need a HTML email client to view this email."

Mind you, I am using a modern HTML–capable email client (hypertext markup language) but the incoming email was not properly formatted.

I could save the email to an .eml file, and then use a plain text editor to read the .eml file to decipher its contents. But why should I do that as a customer or prospect?

HTML emails are visually nicer compared to plain text emails with nothing but a wall of text formed by a monospaced typeface – like comparing a beautiful tapestry to a cement floor.

HTML emails demand more bandwidth than plain text emails, and if done incorrectly, renders the email unreadable to some.

A properly formatted HTML email should conform to the baseline HTML conventions, and provide an alternative plain text version of the email. In this fashion, someone with an email client that cannot read the badly formatted HTML email, will still be able to read your email in plain text.

In most direct marketing campaigns, you may notice the availability of receiving emails in plain text or HTML formats.

However, the option to select such a choice should only be after initial interactions in plain text. This is to prevent sales and interactions blocked due to a technical glitch from your end.

Ask yourself: Are you looking for sales and interactions from your users, or do you just want to stare at an arguably "prettier" email that shuts out some of your prospects?

7 tips to recover from a service failure (hospitality scenario)

What happens when an establishment fails miserably at customer service, because of systems and procedure failures? What can it do to recover from such failures?

I have always been intrigued and interested in business processes and human interaction in business, and service quality, as well as process and total quality management (TQM), naturally became favorite study subjects of mine in my earlier years. Since the 1980s, I took time to research and develop customer service and total quality training programs that were delivered for clients, and also into books.

To me, customer service is not just about good human relations, but depends heavily on having efficient and trouble–free systems and procedures as well. In many front–line scenarios, I have seen the best of human etiquette and courtesy crippled by laggard or dysfunctional systems and procedures.

I was at a newly opened resort hotel for the first time. The hotel had some raving reviews during its launch, and I figured I was in for a nice experience to take some stress off work. Hospitality establishments are important in our business, especially when clients are always demanding for new, thematic and unique MICE (meetings, incentives, conventions, and exhibitions) venues, and depend on us to recommend what kind of establishments to engage for marketing campaigns and events.

This hotel has a very unique and artistic feel to its architecture and design. When we checked in, the process was not fast, and we attributed it to being a newly opened establishment. We completed the procedure and were given keys to a room. We took the elevator and went to the door. When we opened the door, there was something amiss that we couldn't immediately put a finger on.

There was an Apple MacBook on the desk, and we thought it was a complimentary "for–use" laptop for guests. Then we realized something strange. There was a pair of used shorts on the chair, and a half–consumed sports drink. We immediately realized we were assigned a room that has a CURRENT guest. What's worse, there is a bright red stain on the edge of the bed (I could not discern if it was food or something else – and I didn't want to stay another second to find out).

We dashed out of the room and grabbed the floor butler and showed her what happened. The butler and her colleague panicked when they saw the stain on the bed. The butler quickly asked us to wait by the elevator while she scurried to the front desk downstairs to change a new room for us.

After what seemed like a long time, she came back up and apologized profusely and gave us keys to a new room on another floor. Her apology was genuine and we appreciate her prompt action and her apology.

When we got in the room, another surprise awaited us. There was a bowl of cut strawberries there. I presumed (foolishly) that it was perhaps an apology gift for us. We soon realized there was a written card that showed the strawberries were meant for some other people. Someone hurriedly came to collect them with no apology whatsoever.

Then we realized, another unpleasant surprise. The expensive sound system in the main room was not working, and the audio for the TV channels could only be heard from the bathroom. This was not winning any points with us.

During the evening, we saw a letter stuck to our door. It was a letter from the management. It stated that due to an anticipated full house the next day, we were advised to check out an hour earlier than usual (11 am instead of 12 pm).

It was the first time I have ever seen such a letter from a hospitality establishment, large or small, local or foreign (I have traveled to the Americas, Europe, Australasia, and Asia). So, despite a pleasant ambience of the establishment, I can only rate the establishment as an "epic fail" in customer service.

The system in the hotel must have some discrepancies that could not detect if a room is vacated or not. Most hospitality establishments today have sophisticated check–in/out systems that would never assign an occupied room – it is a simple application of business rules management systems (BRMS).

What could a hotel or any establishment of any size, with a commitment to service have done despite system and procedure shortcomings?

1. When something similar happens, **immediately change a room** for the guest, preferably a room that has better amenities, with some reparative measures such as promptly prepared fresh fruits, snacks, a bottle of champagne, and maybe a dinner in the restaurant.

2. Have the **day manager or the general manager personally approach** the guest at an appropriate time and invite the guest to the lounge for a drink on the house, and make some personal conversation to placate and soothe his frayed nerves. This would show that the establishment is truly one with a personal touch and real management attention.

3. When the guest leaves, have some **formal apology mailed** to the guest a couple of days later, and have a genuine expression to the guest that despite the mistakes, the establishment has looked into the system failures and will try its best to do better. And do invite the guest back again.

4. Ensure that an entry of the **service failure incident is noted** in the hotel system so that any attending staff will be extra attentive to prevent any margin of error in the future.

5. Immediately **diagnose and patch** the system and procedure shortcomings to prevent similar failures from potentially happening again in the future. Such failures are easily fixed, with a proper business rules management system (BRMS) to converge business and operational logic into processes. BRMS systems take away human errors and reduce human intervention, catering to specific human intervention should needs arise for out–of–norm circumstances.

6. Ensure that guest **facilities and products actually work** before allowing them to use them. That is the minimum of any service delivery process.

7. **NEVER rescind a contract** with a guest. If a guest paid for a service that says, "Check–out is 12pm," then the check–out is 12 pm, and not unilaterally changed by the establishment as

if the current guest is less important than the next guest. This is a taboo in any service scenario.

These tips can be adapted for any service establishment, and for anyone serving another.

Customer service is not a walk in the park. The hospitality business is ruthlessly competitive and any chance of keeping a customer is an advance against the competition. It is never going to be easy, and humans and systems can all yield errors and mistakes.

It is acceptable and understandable that people will make mistakes. The crux is whether the leadership can take bold moves to retain customers and make mission–critical changes to their system (even if it seems to have worked before, or elsewhere).

Customer service and social media – Think back–end first

Some recent marketers were commenting that social media can be a compelling means to gain more customers through good service. However, the devil is in the details.

Customer service can make or break a brand, and can also derail the most expensive and most creative marketing campaigns if customer service lapses are too tragic. Some people imagine service as an area you can "fix" by simply training front–line employees to be pleasant to customers and placate every request, reasonable or unreasonable.

The rise of social media increases the complexity of service whereby anyone with a social media account on a phone, a tablet or a computer, can communicate requests (however far–fetched) and complaints. People seem to be more willing to voice their complaints online because they feel a sense of anonymity and "safety," hiding behind a keyboard and screen, without a face–to–face confrontation with a service provider, human being to human being, feelings meeting feelings.

Yet, service is not just about having respect and courtesy to customers. It entails the back–end processes and systems.

I have observed, as a process and service quality consultant in my earlier years, that even if front–line employees are willing and happy to be courteous to paying customers, the back–end systems and processes may derail their best practical and emotive efforts, and invariably, demoralize them to quit.

Imagine this. If a famous brand has poor or missing inventory control and supply chain systems, with crippling workflow processes that impede the progress and the empowerment of front–line employees, any courtesy or smile extended to paying customers will be utterly useless, because orders cannot be fulfilled, sales are lost, repairs or replacements can't be adequately addressed, and so on.

Marketing is seductive because it is front–facing to the public, and companies may be more easily persuaded to put priority in that area. However, it is equally important to have a working, or better yet, a compelling supply chain and workflow system that lubricates the entire sales and support process (e.g. enterprise resource planning or ERP), such that every order is fulfilled, every request easily relayed and answered promptly, and every stakeholder in the workflow process adequately informed on time, with a dashboard access. This is not some pipe dream or science fiction. Many successful companies have all these in place. Yet, there are still companies struggling along without well integrated back–end systems and workflow processes.

Customer service is not a bandage or an afterthought. It should be tightly integrated with the entire workflow and the supply chain process. No amount of creative marketing firepower can rescue dysfunctional back–ends, and tragically, customer service lapses will then become a chronic condition.

Therefore, while teams are working on great marketing campaigns or exciting product development, remember to look into work processes and the supply chain too.

Grooming authentic salespeople

Good salespeople are not about ruthless aggression. Truly great salespeople have unique qualities that endear them to customers and their companies alike. What makes them great?

I read of a great story about putting salespeople to experience the very products they sell in a bootcamp. One salesperson came out of the experience very enthusiastic about the kitchen appliance product, having found ways to use the product to create food that he liked. That salesperson could thereafter recount his personal experiences to every contact he met, and persuade them to buy his products, simply because he was genuine and really knew what his products could do and mean to another person.

All too often, salespeople are measured by performance figures. Such targeted numbers are created by some leaders who may not even have been in the field at all. Some leaders may have lost touch with the field altogether having been away from hands–on field work for years or decades, and the field is an entirely different one today.

Just a decade ago, many things evolved at a glacial pace. The last few years have seen colossal and quantum leap changes to every facet of our lives. Having lost touch with the field just from the last few years, would render a person completely detached from every shred of reality in the world. Therefore, unless the leaders understand the field from a truly hands–on perspective, their own concoctions of targets and performance indicators are simply wishes. Leaders have to be as authentic and realistic as the demands they impose on salespeople. Better yet, leaders should brave the field with their salespeople, side by side, or lead them into the battle for performance.

As a passionate human capital practitioner for more than two decades, I have also seen the waves of various methods and ideas behind sales training programs. I have seen many sales training programs targeted at either merely providing facts, specifications, and selling points of products, or are geared towards creating a euphoric feeling in the salespeople and hope that such temporarily induced euphoria can be carried out in the field, and wishfully forever.

However, the reality is that many sales training programs will not produce better salespeople, and may dissuade many people from wanting to develop a sales career altogether.

A great development program should be one to sieve out the right people for the right jobs, and then to inspire them to explore, learn, experiment, ask questions, develop solutions for every challenge, face the challenges head on, perhaps fail occasionally, and allow them to pick up the pieces and start again. Humans, especially salespeople, are best inspired, and given every opportunity to invoke their curiosity to learn and solve problems on their own. Therefore, the best development programs inspire and engage learners to draw out their own qualities to the maximum.

Most importantly, allow salespeople to immerse in the products and experience them firsthand as customers and users. If you are selling a computer, have the salesperson use the computer in every way possible. If you are selling a kitchen appliance, have the salesperson use it at home or at work, daily if possible. If you are selling a software solution, whether enterprise or consumer, have the salesperson use it and explore every feature and discover every possible benefit. Nothing beats using a product for real, and experiencing the product for all its advantages and disadvantages. The salesperson will then be able to share his experience with prospects and customers with an authentic and persuasive delivery. This will allow the salesperson to be genuine with the customers, and the customers will appreciate the honesty, the realities, and be emotively engaged to make more preferential decisions.

The best way to groom salespeople for greatness, is to lead by example, and to immerse in the field together with them. Business, as with war, is a reality that must be engaged and experienced firsthand, and over time. No business can be managed in a vacuum, on a computer screen, or through a simulation. Battles in business are real, get hands-on, get real.

dot zen 2.0

Branding & Reputation

7 tips of a good brand name

When you think of a great brand, what pops to your mind?

For example, when you think of personal computers, some immediate brand names would appear in our thought bubbles – Apple, Dell, Lenovo, and HP. When you think of smartphones, again, names such as Apple's iPhone, Samsung, HTC, BlackBerry, Sony might appear. And when we think of automobiles, brands such as Toyota, Audi, VW, Mercedes–Benz, and BMW, may spring to mind.

The brand name recognition of these companies have formed in our minds, through the companies' consistent and disciplined approach to communicating, persuading, and educating us through a long time.

Recently, I was reading an industry magazine. The editors conducted a tiny experiment to show that even the best search engines can produce mediocre or even hilarious results, especially when you type in a very common name. What does that have to do with branding?

Imagine if you name your company or products with "me too" names shared with many others.

First, you would not be able to register those names as they could be too generic to be registered as trademarks.

Second, you would be drowned in a flood of similarly named products and brands.

Just as the Internet domain registration craze has come and gone, we need to retain sanity when choosing names. Just because we want to stand out in the crowded space of many "me too" products, naming our products with unpronounceable and utterly weird names, would not make sense either.

Therefore, when you are naming the latest gadget or your new company, it is important to have names that are:

1. Unique,

2. Pronounceable,

3. Contextually cognitive,

4. Memorable,

5. Trademark–able,

6. Emotive, and

7. Short on letters and syllables.

A name can invoke emotions, and create a personality that allows your imagination to take over.

For example, does the name make you imagine the company to be professional? Does the name make you imagine a product to execute particular functions? Do you feel an emotive bond with the name because it invokes a visual imagery you have a personal experience with?

So, if you have named your product or company well, let's hope that the next time you, a customer, or a trade partner, will find most of the links on search engines, pointing to you.

Do you get design or do you go cheap?

Let's face it, the best brands in the world, such as the iconic Apple, Nike, Starbucks, Sony, and so on, have iconic product designs that are not smashed together randomly nor done cheaply. Their designs are culminated from serious commitment (that also means financial commitment) to human factors, elegance, and simplicity.

 Fast Company (fastcompany.com), one of my favorite business magazines, did a feature article on the state of design in their Oct 2011 issue. It was a great read, and the Apple Mac came to mind.

When you trace the lineage of the Mac, you would notice that the user interface is made to be elegantly simple. That kind of interface did not come from one afternoon of coding.

Likewise, from their entire line of colorful iMacs, to the white iBooks, to the later models such as MacBooks and MacMinis, and then the iPhone and other iOS devices, all of them visually and innately displayed the great application of human factors engineering (or "ergonomics") from the software to to the hardware alike.

Many of the top brands in the world spent millions of dollars to put product design as important as features, specifications, and functionality.

We are not talking about just the pretty packaging some products go by, but the serious industrial design of the products, so that they are usable, elegant, attractive, and most of all, can be manufactured without trouble. It is a specialized field that has to be left in the hands of passionate professionals.

What does great design do for a product? In a word – sales.

The increasingly demanding customers today are not going to be happy simply with cheap, or cheap–looking products. The increasing sophistication of the consumer landscape means that they are looking for a holistic engagement and interaction experience with your brand. Your product may be made affordably, but it certainly cannot look or feel cheap.

Behind the greatest industrial designs often also lies great manufacturing, that can deliver nice–looking products at decent prices.

So when building a brand, remember that the best brands, often your most terrifying competitors, are not giving in to a cavalier treatment of industrial design and packaging design. They are treating design as one of the pillars of a successful product. Do you?

Advent of "brand journalism"

The media landscape is blurring, with blogging, social media, online video, and now, "brand journalism." It sure seems dizzying for practitioners and journalists alike.

I have been on all sides of the fence — as an accredited journalist reporting news for broadcast and print, a technology commentator and analyst, as well as a marketer and publicist.

All sides are stimulating and challenging, and increasingly, made even more challenging with citizen journalism and social media thrown in the mix. And now there is "brand journalism."

As a journalist and commentator inclined towards objective reporting and analyses, my first knee–jerk reaction to the concept of "brand journalism" might have been skepticism. Some of us might just call it as it should be – public relations.

Yet, as someone on the other side of the fence, I might find the concept of "brand journalism" somewhat enticing. It may have a commercial slant, but it may just mean that we have to work harder to make such content acceptable to readers. In short, as marketers, we may have to begin to think like a journalist.

How should companies grapple with brand journalism and do it acceptably to the discerning public? And what are the pitfalls to avoid? Lewis DVorkin commented that it might be good for the news business with the emergence of brand journalism.

In a nutshell, brand journalism, or perhaps "PR 21st" (as in "public relations in the twenty–first century"), can help traditional media become more conscious and conscientious than ever before.

The public are warming up to the use of the social media and even citizen journalism sources as sources of information, and sometimes circumventing traditional media altogether. The rise of the mobile and tablet space is also changing how the public retrieve news and other information.

It is no wonder almost every traditional media source (print and broadcast alike) are also going to the mobile app space (whether native or Web–based).

One thing marketers must have no illusions about, is "brand journalism," whatever its label may be, will find some skepticism and resistance from mainstream media.

However, one of the things marketers can do is to present the information in as much a journalistic style as mainstream media, following as much as possible the same heights of ethical and quality standards. This makes the presentation accountable to ourselves, as well as to the public, who would come to expect accurate, objective, useful and entertaining information, just as they would expect the same from traditional sources.

 One great example is Cisco, the network technology vendor. They did not set out to compete with traditional media, but simply to create engaging content that would interact with their users and stakeholders. The result is a great site known as "Cisco Newsroom: The Network", which taps on engaging videos about relevant technology adoption, produced in a manner that has immediacy, relevance, and high–quality production values.

Next, marketers may need to realize, that setting up such content and Web properties may mean serious commitment to production, on a sustained manner.

One simply cannot produce a few and then give up. Social media engagement relies on a continuous and sustainable process much like public relations (PR). Social media and in this case, "brand journalism," are very unlike advertising which can be short bursts of exciting campaigns.

So, marketers need to keep pace, and keep up with the ongoing development of quality and engaging content for this space to keep users engaged on a long–term basis. If at first it makes sense to engage third parties to produce the content, do so. If the company feels the need to develop an in–house team, do so, seriously as well. The kind of equipment is not trivial. If you are putting together a roving crew and setup, you are looking at HD DSLR or HD video gear, and maybe even chromakey screens and desktop editing suites, with good and extensible data storage to keep your footage and edited content, and maybe even offload to the cloud for archival.

Third, do something different from the mainstream media. For a company, instead of simply producing b—rolls of the same content that would have been sent to the media, why not consider producing educational and entertaining short films that have "viral" built into them. These films can have subtle hints of the products of the company, but would be fast—paced, emotive, and have a good storyline.

This is certainly not something that one can hack together over a weekend, but might require professional assistance to put together, including writers, editors, camera crew, post—production crew, etc. Two automobile brands, Audi and Nissan, have both created superlative cinematic—quality videos with great production values and engaging stories. They were not low—cost productions, but were compelling, viral and in my opinion, worth every penny of investment.

As a marketer, we may not necessarily pursue the idea of "brand journalism" to the fullest extent as some of these companies had, but it is something we need to keep in mind when progressing with our marketing programs, or as publicists who need to give timely and relevant counsel to clients. It is a phenomenon we cannot ignore, and yet, demand a great deal out of us, financially, physically, and infrastructure—wise. Take time to study what can be done, what needs to be done, and how best to approach this idea moving forward.

May you have fun engaging your audience!

3 tips of rebuilding trust with your customers

Your brand's reputation is not about the bells and whistles of your products and associated technologies, or the glitzy marketing campaigns. It is much simpler.

Our firm has gone through constant reengineering to adapt to changing needs of communication, so that clients are always served with the most relevant forms of communication outreach to the media and other stakeholders.

So, we have gone full circle to bring back video as a mainstream media outreach tool again. The last time we used video full–time as a means of corporate communication was in the mid to late 1990s, when nonlinear editing just began on the consumer desktop (remember AVID Media Suite Pro and Adobe Premiere 1.0?) These days, 1080p HD video and nonlinear editing are common, and the online video phenomenon has cemented the need for video as a serious communication medium, complementary to textual news and content.

I have gone on to embrace DSLR filmmaking as the main means of creating HD video, which works out great. I use the Olympus and Panasonic micro four–third (MFT) cameras with interchangeable lenses, which worked very well in the field, whether in blazing hot weather, or indoors. I have used such MFT HD DSLR systems successfully to produce video news releases (VNRs), live event recording, and even live–streaming for clients, with these cameras mounted on rigs and stabilization gear.

More recently, I decided to buy a semi–professional HD video camera system from a name brand vendor, potentially as a video camera for long events, since video cameras can use large capacity batteries that may not be readily available for MFT HD DSLR systems (there are some custom solutions, but are OEM rather than from the original vendors).

There was a wide–angle zoom lens that I bought for the video camera just a month ago, and used for a test shoot only once. Over the weekend, I brought out the lens and mated to the video camera and thought of experimenting with shoots over the weekend. When I turned on the video camera, a strange whirring sound came about, and an error notification came on, and the iris would not open, yielding a dark image that was unusable. I mated the video camera to another zoom lens, and it worked perfectly.

I brought the lens to the authorized service center and explained the situation, and the junior front–liner took the lens and tried it on the center's camera, and it seemed to work. He mated the lens back on my own video camera and it seemed to work. However, because this lens and video camera is meant for professional shoots and NOT a hobby tool, any sign of even a single failure means that I cannot take a chance. Imagine shooting a live client event and have the lens fail on me, and the client's faith would be lost, and I would have failed the client because the lens chooses to fail then. It is unacceptable.

Therefore, I explained to the junior front–liner that this lens needs to be exchanged with another lens as a replacement. The front–liner had the most intolerable expression on his face and insisted that no exchange can be made. I stormed out of the service center.

To me, this video camera is no longer worthy to be used for professional shoots, and I would relegate it as a toy in a corner and used when I feel like it. I cannot stake my reputation and my client's very important needs on a tool that may just malfunction at the wrong time. My confidence as a consumer is erased, and is unlikely to be restored simply because the vendor's junior staffer refused to recognize the importance of a simple exchange of a faulty product. Confidence from a consumer is not easily earned, and is easily lost.

I will therefore invest in what I already own, in the MFT HD DSLR systems which have not failed me in tough shooting situations.

What could a vendor have done? The product was bought recently, and is meant for professional work. The vendor should:

1. **Develop front–line employees to be patient**, and especially, to only recruit people who are empathetic to the needs of others. Those without empathy have no business serving customers directly at the front–line.

2. **Empower front–line employees to make good judgment** calls to exercise product exchanges or loans until products are properly diagnosed and repaired, and refunds when necessary. If front–line employees cannot be empowered for some reason, have field managers on hand to immediately resolve such issues and make the right judgment calls in favor of customers.

3. **Follow through with customers** who face product failures and issues, to ensure that confidence can be restored, and continue to keep in touch with such customers. After all, even customers who face problems with your products are capable to be won back by your empathy and good follow–through service, and can eventually even be your evangelists.

The world is getting smaller, and the market getting more competitive. Winning a new customer is tough, and keeping one is easier if you make even the smallest effort. Recovering a customer who faces problems with your products, become paramount to keeping existing customers and potentially winning new ones through word–of–mouth evangelism.

Isn't it worth every bit of your time, effort and resources to keep your hard–earned customers?

dot zen 2.0

Marketing

What's your "out of box" experience?

Many years back, I bought the LG Chocolate mobile phone. More recently, I bought the Fujifilm X100 camera. What made these two products stand out?

It has to do with the "out of box" experience.

When you open the packaging of the LG Chocolate phone and the Fujifilm X100 camera, you are wowed by the luxurious feel and colors of the packaging. When you open the packaging of one of these products, you really feel that you are unwrapping a beautiful gift from a loved one.

Conversely, many top global brands have simplified their packaging and removed or reduced the "wow" from opening the products and the packaging.

While simplification is often a good thing, the commoditized nature of many consumer products means that it will get more challenging to entice and excite consumers before these products are unwrapped and actually used.

While packaging costs money for sure, consumers must not feel as if they are paying a premium just for packaging. The products should outperform equivalent products, so that you feel "wowed." Otherwise, they will feel that they are merely paying for a "me–too" product at elevated prices.

What are you really offering a corporate sponsor?

Every other day, we get bombarded with a request for sponsorship from a student somewhere, for our clients or our firm. However, rather than simply asking for something, what is it you are really offering a sponsor?

Asking for money or something in kind is easy. You simply ask. However, discerning what is in it for your potential sponsor and making the return on investment (ROI) really compelling for your sponsor, that is the question.

Often, a typical student approaching an organization asking for cash is simply promising a mention in an internal collateral that is circulated to the faculty or the institution. How the collateral is really distributed, actively, or more likely, passively, is seldom communicated to the potential sponsor.

If you have been a college student before, you would, like me, not really notice the fine print about who were the sponsors for a student event. You would more likely look at the notice board for something interesting (if you are really bored), and then simply jot down the details and attend the event.

Therefore, if that's the great pitch, then you cannot expect much from a sponsor. If however, you plan for an event that is actively and persuasively communicated to a massive audience, especially through proven past media coverage to the mainstream broadcast, print and online media (and we are not talking about a friend's social media page), then the sponsor would more likely sit up and listen.

Second, what is usually said to the potential sponsor is a speculative number of attendees, and worse, the number is not compelling either. The pitch usually may mention a potential future customer base, which when mapped to the actual event, may not necessarily correlate to real prospects.

Let's use a fictitious example. If you are organizing a student event for rock climbers, and you send a pitch randomly to many potential sponsors such as restaurants, hotels or spas, the correlation is really low. But if, for this fictitious example, you target only relevant companies in extreme sports apparel, portable video cameras, sports recovery drinks and nutrition products, then it would make perfect sense.

Next, what is the promised and realistic ROI your potential sponsor can expect? Is there something tangible, believable and achievable? If you ask for US$1,000 from your sponsor, what can your sponsor expect in return? Think about it. Think really hard. And then, prove it to your sponsor. If you cannot, ask for less, or in–kind. Or get creative.

For example, if you have permission to use a space for your event (from your college or a regulatory authority), you may be permitted to allow potential sponsors to set up shop in parts of the space and ask for a small fee as sponsorship. That may make it more compelling especially for FMCG sponsors.

Sponsors are not charities, and what one asks for, sponsors expect an achievable and a great ROI. It is perfectly alright to be realistic and modest. There is nothing wrong from starting from the ground up. All great things start with a good foundation.

4 marketing tips from a Korean hit song

Korean Rap singer Psy has hit all the airwaves and stations with his recent hit Gangnam Style. What can we learn from his hit song in branding and marketing?

You may have heard and seen the quirky, catchy and enjoyable Korean song – "Gangnam Style," by Korean rap singer Psy. Unlike many Korean pop groups and singers who are younger, Psy is an average middle–aged gentleman. Other than his strong masculine vocals, why did  his song catch on? And more congruent to our business, what can we learn from his song's popularity that we can learn for branding and marketing? Surprisingly, at least four things:

1. **Window dressing is not everything**. In the fast–moving consumer goods (FMCG) industry, we often imagine retail outlets having the best visual merchandising, the grandest and most expensive displays, and the most flashy front–line staff uniforms and so on, would beat the plain old store with simple layouts and down–to–earth apparels for employees. After all, there are some who would argue that looks mean everything. However, in the case of Psy, his confidence, his vocals, his soulful rendition, and his humor, all stood shoulder to shoulder with other competing Korean pop groups or singers with better packaging. It is therefore important that we remember content and substance mean everything. When we develop our core competencies, our

knowledge, our business intelligence, our corporate personality, we may compete easily with others with a much bigger budget spent on visual packaging. Customers are buying an experience and a quality product. A quality product is a given. An experience does not however, necessarily mean an expensive window display or store decor, but how knowledgeable, approachable, sensitive and persuasive the front–line employees are to the customer. All too often, we have walked into an expensive outlet only to have front–liners who tend to us with little or no professional knowledge, failing us miserably, and leaving us to figure out just what we want and need.

2. **Make things simple and make them work**. Psy's song has a simple premise – a happy and humorous song with simple lyrics that are catchy and easy to remember, an even simpler dance routine that anyone can emulate and enjoy. Psy has literally moved internationally, having gone on to entertain  and teach his simple dance to top global celebrities and personalities alike (even the Honorable Ban Ki–Moon, United Nations secretary general!). Therefore, in our marketing and branding efforts, let us try to be radically and compellingly succinct in our brand and product messaging, slogans, advertising copy, news releases, technical and usage documentation, usage mechanics and workflow, and most of all, the product must simply just work, without bewildering our customers. There is a reason why certain products moved more pervasively in the market, such as OS X, iOS devices, Ubuntu Linux, and now, Windows 8.

3. **Let us entertain our customers**. If you have used YouTube, you would notice that the most popular videos, even if they have a commercial bent, are those that are deeply entertaining or downright hilarious. Against the economic woes the world endures, what many of us would like is some harmless entertainment anyone can enjoy to lighten the nerves we shoulder daily. Psy has created an entertaining phenomenon of a song, that has rolled so many in laughter that many even parodied his song worldwide – a sure sign of a successful viral phenomenon. Likewise, when we entertain our customers, keep our videos short (thirty seconds to one minute), keep them decent and hilarious (fit for anyone from a young kid to a mature adult), and keep our messaging memorable (and provide a link if possible).

4. **Build compelling partnerships**. Psy has partnered with popular singers, a great ensemble of dancers and actors, and a stable of horses, to deliver a powerful rendition of a grand music and dance experience in his music video. If Psy merely sang and danced by himself, the song would have had less traction. In business, find honorable and complementary partners to work with, to build on areas we are deficient in (by choice or not), so that we can offer holistic and comprehensive services to serve the needs of our customers.

The world is competitive, and complementary partners help each other build far more successful businesses than each one can do by itself. When we build our brands, the best marketing efforts tend to have substance, simple and functional, positively entertaining, and leverage on the collective strengths of many. May our brands sizzle and dazzle our customers!

Marketing is about strategy, not mere tactics

When you think about marketing, is it merely the dictionary definition of providing goods or services to satisfy customer needs? Or something much more?

On the surface, the field of marketing is to meet customer needs through the provision of goods and services. It is a sophisticated and still evolving professional field that integrates many synergistic activities together to bring about the desired end results for both sellers and buyers.

These activities can include promotional activities that would stimulate the selling process, such as advertising, direct marketing, events, public relations, social media, mobile apps, research, etc.

Beyond tactical activities, sound marketing should really be about creating a strategy that would not just propel a product or service into the market with excitement and attraction that would immediately engage the buying interests of consumers, and should sustain the company, its brands, products and services for the long haul.

After all, a company is not a temporary project, but something that deserves sufficient longevity, if at least to lend traction to its brands, imprinting some degree of permanence in consumers' minds and hearts.

The word "strategy" is derived from the Greek word "strategia," which means "the office or the command of a general."

Therefore, when you think of a general commanding a sizable army, you know at once, a general thinks through his plans that would protect the territorial rights and privileges, cater to the immediate needs of his people and those he protects, as well as cater to the farther needs of the population.

In short, a sound strategy is a continuous program that protects and nurtures the entire timeline of existence from the "now" to the "far future." It is not a transient or temporary fix.

Online advertising is on the rise, as it is one of the advertising media with simpler points of entry compared to more elaborate and traditional campaigns. With the advent of social media, targeted online advertising to social media channels is also accelerating for companies  hoping to tap into the millions of social media users. But social media is not without caveats. Not all users may be actual humans, and duplicates may exist, creating a possible opacity to targeted online advertising campaigns in some cases (BBC).

To some marketers, online advertising through various online platforms (whether search engines or social media channels) can be a short–term fix to bringing awareness to their products and services.

However, as we read from various media commentaries, it becomes clear that online advertising is NOT a strategy – it is merely yet another tactical approach in the pie of tactical approaches such as print and broadcast advertising, direct marketing, events and so on. Sometimes, online advertising may not even be the most effective approach, or at all. Online advertising must be part of a greater strategy and program, and not naively perceived as the panacea to end all other marketing approaches and tactics.

To bring positive mindshare to the market for your brands, products or services, consider FIRST, the need for expertise to crystalize a strategy (whether in–house, or a field–tested consulting partner) that would bring sustainable positive change for your brands, products and services.

This is not just about publicity and marketing campaign strategies, but can entail business plans, elevator pitch preparation, market research, branding and positioning, audiovisual presentations, etc.

You may be a business owner, or you may be a rising star in your organization. No single platform or tactic can solve the entire marketing puzzle for you. Look at your marketing journey as a successful expedition, and not a brilliant spark that fizzles out the next second.

The secret to great marketing can be found in fried rice

The common Yangzhou fried rice is a staple in many Chinese restaurants and small eateries. Yet, within the seemingly simple dish embodies some of the greatest strengths of Chinese wok cooking. What has fried rice got to do with marketing?

Yangzhou fried rice is not really a dish from Yangzhou, mainland China, but was created by Qing Dynasty's Yi Bingshou (1754 to 1815 AD), who was a magistrate of Yangzhou at one time.

What is Yangzhou fried rice, for the uninitiated? It is a dish with cooked rice, char siew (barbecued pork), cooked or fried shrimp, finely chopped spring onions, and egg yolk.

A good plate of Yangzhou fried rice must have distinct rice grains that are not clumped together, and each grain should have a fine coating of egg yolk, just sufficiently so, and the dish must not taste soggy or oily. There is an incredible fragrance of the mixture of all these common ingredients together that makes this dish memorable when done right.

Many of us have tried our hands at frying a wok of Yangzhou fried rice, but the master chefs would let you know that it is one of the seemingly most mundane dishes that demand real decades of solid cooking experience. It is not a dish you can just whip up without field experience.

In marketing, let us remember that it is also like a good dish of Yangzhou fried rice. It is a discipline best done repeatedly, field–

tested ad infinitum in the heat and blasts of the battlefields of the marketplace.

Marketing is not a field for the novice to command, and it requires humility, practice, constant learning, and most of all, a consolidation of core strengths of various components that make the sum so much greater than the mere parts.

Each of the ingredients in Yangzhou fried rice are simple, and yet, each demands some careful preparation. The shrimp has to be properly cleaned and de-shelled and cooked just sufficiently. The char siew is another science in itself, requiring marinating, cooking and frying, and dicing to small bits. The spring onions has to be finely chopped so that the fragrance can blossom during wok frying, without overpowering the taste of the whole dish. The rice is not something to be cavalier either, sometimes requiring the storage of cooked rice overnight before using it.

In marketing, the parts can be public relations, social media, advertising, direct marketing, events, mobile marketing, internal communication, crisis prevention, market research, and so on. There are many components, and none of them should overpower the others, and they must have a broad umbrella strategy (akin to the wok, frying temperature, and skills) that brings all these components elegantly together to create a marketing machinery far greater than each of the marketing tactics and channels.

The next time you sit down with a good plate of Yangzhou fried rice, remember that we marketers are just like the master chefs who needed decades of experience behind them, slaving in the kitchen for long hours of toil, to arrive at creating the perfect Yangzhou fried rice, a memorable taste that is at once so deceivingly simple, and yet so emotively compelling that it moves us.

Make magic happen, but remember behind every magic is a painfully built set of core strengths from tears and sweat of hard work.

Chinese painting and what it means to marketing

Having been a trained Chinese painter since my teenage years, it struck me one day when juggling various ideas in my head, that there is some resonance between Chinese painting and the fields of branding and marketing. How?

There are two distinct styles of Chinese painting, both of which I was schooled in.

There is a meticulous, fine–stroked approach known as "gong bi" (loosely translated as "detailed brush"). You may see some of these paintings in museums and art galleries, where every detail is painted with fine brushes and are usually colorful, and the paintings are more literal in expression. The tenth century artist Gu Hongzhong was known for the "gong bi" style.

There is another, known as "shui mo" (loosely translated as "water and ink"), or "xie yi" (loosely translated as "freestyle"), which is a free, expressive, bold and broad strokes approach, where the paintings tend to be more figurative. Colors tend to be lighter. The twentieth century artist Xu Beihong is known for the "xie yi" style.

I have a personal bias for the "xie yi" approach, because I am expressive and bold, and do not care too much for spending more time that I like to communicate an idea. With the "xie yi" approach, I could easily paint what I hope to convey, in broad and bold strokes with bold thick brushes, with just sufficient strokes and shades to give the viewer mental space and latitude, giving him ownership of what he would perceive from the painting.

Mind you, the "xie yi" approach is not abstract art. It is a bold and minimalist approach to communicating a visual idea. So, what has "xie yi" painting got to do with branding and marketing? In my humble opinion, a lot, especially since time is a precious commodity, and the attention span of people can be very short.

There is a Chinese proverb, "hua she tian zu," or "drawing legs for a snake," which can be translated to mean doing redundant things that have no value for anything.

Likewise, in branding and marketing, sometimes we must watch over ourselves or over our clients, so that none of us do more than it is necessary to communicate an idea well.

 The analogy can be seen in the best minimalist designs in the modern world – the likes of Apple Macs and iOS devices, Audi automobiles, Nikon 1 cameras, Nespresso coffee machines, the new Microsoft Windows 8, and so on.

All of these products have clean minimalist lines without extraneous details that are redundant to distract the visual flow of the products, with ergonomics par excellence.

So when it comes to branding, we need to define and refine our brand to the bare fundamentals, that of communicating very succinctly what we represent. This would mean our logo, our visual identity, our product designs, and so on. Distill our brand down to something iconic.

For example, you may be familiar with the Apple logo today. But do you recall how the first Apple logo look like?

It was a rather complex illustration, and was not exactly what I would consider an iconic design. The logo went through several iterations, before it arrives at the monochromatic apple with a leaf and a bitten off corner. It is as classic and as iconic as a logo can go.

As for marketing, the same rules apply. Think about how your marketing programs and campaigns can be, and then distill them down to the bare fundamentals that would communicate your key message well. Keep refining, keep thinking, keep being harsh to your own developments until you can call it "fundamental" or even "iconic."

We Chinese have a saying, "slow and steady labor produces the finest work." May your brand and your marketing campaigns reach new heights, with the simplest and most elegant of ideas and expressions.

Optimizing paid, earned and owned media

As strategists and executives continue to hone their media usage from a largely paid media use, to an increasing spread of earned and owned media, what can marketers do to optimize their media spread in the paid, earned and owned spaces?

Already, we can see from published figures from analysts, as well as some projections, that paid media use is declining, against the earned and owned media slices. Marketers are beginning to tighten the spending on paid media, which even against the economic downturn, is not necessarily getting more affordable. It is not because paid media is getting less useful, but sometimes, simply because marketers are facing increasing budgetary pressures, against ever–escalating performance indicators their bosses demand.

Therefore, as marketers, what do we do to optimize what we can afford to spend, in the 3 slices of paid, earned and owned media? First, let us define what paid, earned and owned media are in our marketing context.

1. **Owned media** are what we can control, especially if completely. Owned media can be our website, micro–sites for specific campaigns, mobile sites (or simply websites with "responsive" designs), blogs, and to a lesser extend, some social content on third–party sites that we manage. Owned media can be cost–effective, and we can extend the reach of the content as long as we like, with specific content for specific readers. The flip side of owned media is that it is a

biased medium, and consumers will take time to trust such a medium. Owned media also demands much more from a company, as technical and human capital need to be invested, not sporadically, but for the long haul. There is also no certainty to the acceptance and reach to such content.

2. **Paid media**, in the simplest form, is advertising. Paid media can be advertising in print, in broadcast, online, and outdoors. It can be advertising spent in search channels. Paid media is also sponsorships which involve monetary investments. Paid media is understood to be biased, since it is media we place as marketers for our companies. The media also faces pressure from similar and competing campaigns in the same media space, and consumers increasingly experience fatigue to traditional paid media, and sometimes simply "switch off." Paid media offers marketers direct communication in a controllable timeframe in terms of execution, and can have call–to–action mechanisms.

3. **Earned media** is traditionally what public relations (PR) practitioners specialize in, gaining editorial coverage in the media for clients. Earned media, increasingly, also include any "word–of–mouth" and viral communication by customers, advocates, the media, or the public. Earned media is especially seen in social media and online video channels. Earned media is seen as more credible, since it is said and communicated by third parties, whether by the media, or by the public. The flip side is that we as marketers cannot manage the results, and the mention can sometimes be negative. It is also harder to work in call–to–action mechanisms, since the media itself tend to be unbiased.

Having defined briefly paid, earned and owned media, what should we do as marketers to maximize what we can spend?

For **paid media**, we need to recognize that advertising is not going away. Advertising is evolving, rapidly, and moving from merely clever textual ads in print, to increasingly sophisticated online video advertising that can be interactive. There are also advanced augmented reality advertising campaigns that consumers can interact with through print, outdoors, and online campaigns, complete with videos and Web content (talk to us if you need to understand augmented reality advertising campaigns). Paid media, because of the many conflicting and competing campaigns at the same time, forces us as marketers to become more innovative, more creative, more results–driven, and more discerning based on what and where we spend our advertising dollars. **Be adventurous.**

For **earned media**, we need to look beyond simply hoping for coverage in the media. We need to raise the bar to help our brands elevate above the fray of the competition. There may be rants and brickbats against our brands, and we need to address the concerns and complaints in an open, aboveboard, welcoming, sincere manner. Nobody is perfect, and any entity (such as a company) will be prone to make mistakes. Admit to mistakes promptly, and look for remedial actions that will solve such problems, and work to earn the trust of consumers back over the long haul. We need to understand earned media as not merely media coverage in traditional media, but also, what the greater population can say about our brands to each other. It will be tough, and it will demand a great deal of understanding the social media channels and how they work. Social media channels are not advertising channels to hawk our wares like we might on paid media. Rather, social media channels are about engagement and open communication. Spend time and effort to build up open communication, and have a well–defined social media communication policy and program. Hire people suited for such roles. **Keep going**.

For **owned media**, more can be done to go way beyond merely having a website. A well–designed website is good, but having consistent, useful, and shareable information published for the long haul, better. People are bored with mere "brochureware" websites. The website today has to be content–rich, with rich media content (such as online videos that are "edutaining"). Owned media will not merely be a single corporate website, but has to be a wide spectrum of campaign–specific micro–sites, mobile–friendly content (through native, hybrid, or responsive Web apps), which are automatically or thematically streamed to your social media channels. Owned media becomes the satellite hub for which all content should stem from, and increasingly, can be the source of all news and content delivery to your earned media outreach, and even integrated seamlessly with your paid media campaigns. **Build tenaciously**.

It is no longer a simple path for marketers today. For marketers, we need to understand how much we have in our pockets, and how to spread those dollars to the 3 slices of paid, earned, and owned media. More important, we need to build up our owned media for the long haul to become the hub from which many outreach and marketing campaigns can develop from. May you have a fruitful journey!

Public Relations

5 things to humanize your brand

Public relations is about bringing your brand closer to all your stakeholders. How do we do that? In a nutshell, **HUMANIZE your brand**.

People are drawn to emotions. They feel, and then justify with reasons. People are drawn to other people, and enjoy good interactions with each other. Very few people are drawn simply to facts and numbers, and cold, hard technical specifications. The best evangelists and marketers are those who draw out the positive emotions from people, rather than bore people with details and facts. Who represents such an epitome of drawing people to a brand? Many people may spring to mind, but the late Steve Jobs would be an immediate example. Steve brought Apple and the brand alive, engaging not just the loyal geeks (like me) to the brand and its slew of products, but also just about anyone out there. Apple's consistent success from those times proved that humanizing a brand made a real difference to the bottom line.

Likewise, as marketers and publicity practitioners, we want to bring real people behind your organization and stakeholders to the forefront, and allow your stakeholders, whether the public or the media, to become familiar with them.

We want to bring the human and humane side of your organization to the forefront. We want the public and the media, to see beyond technology, features, facts and figures, to see what a difference your organization makes in the real world, such as your corporate social responsibility (CSR) efforts, and social enterprise projects.

The communication program will attempt to reach the 5 categories of:

1. **TEC** (your technical expertise)

2. **HMN** (human interest areas)

3. **MAC** (macro and sustainability areas)

4. **CUS** (customer care), and

5. **COM** (community involvement).

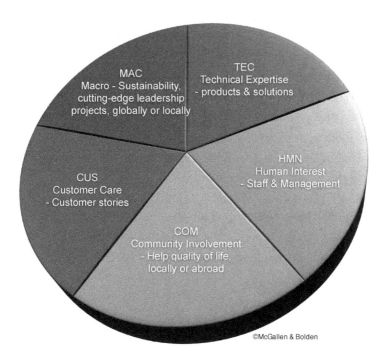

At different times, and depending on the timeliness and the needs of the media and other stakeholders, targeted methods to engage the media and other public stakeholders will be used. This is intended to maximize the media and the public stakeholder outreach.

For news releases, case studies, white papers, and online news, it is wise to present your organization in as many of the areas as possible, whether in trade news, in technical and innovation stories, in end–user customer success stories, in human interest stories, in staffing and appointment news, in community development, in ecological and sustainability stories, and so on.

Public relations is not just about sending a news release or two to an ocean of journalists, and hoping for a slice of media coverage. Just as a person shows a complex and multifaceted personality, the best public relations for a brand is also complex and multifaceted, with a spectrum of news presentations and possibilities, to draw in and engage audiences out there, to show the human side of the brand.

Take your brand and open it up and show its heart and soul to the world. And when you can bring a human heart and soul to your brand, you would have found what a difference your brand can make to the world.

Public Relations? No, much more!

One of the largest public relations firms renamed to make clear that it manages much more than public relations, and includes digital communications. That is necessary and wise.

When we started in the mid 1990s, we recognized then that communications for clients cannot be restricted to merely media relations, but needed quality internal communications as well.

Since then, we delivered quality public relations counsel to clients, and also provided complementary tactical approaches such website development, curriculum development, training, and human resource consulting for clients.

When you think about it, every employee within a company is a spokesperson and public representative for a company, just as much as officially designated spokespersons are. If every employee understands what the company stands for, knows the company's products well, knows how to relay information to stakeholders and executives within the company when required, will invariably ensure the continued success for this company, strengthening the company much more than a few spokespersons can do.

Conversely, if an entire company's employees are not knowledgeable and have no regard for public or media queries, they will become a stumbling block to a company, whether the company faces a real world crisis or not. Compounding this challenge is the ever–evolving landscape for communications. It is a challenge to keep pace, and yet it is not something that can be ignored by every internal stakeholder of a company.

As soon as social media began to emerge on the radar screen, clients began to enquire if we can provide social media and mobile application consulting. The tools and technologies may differ from an average public relations arsenal, but the client requirement to reach out to the audiences out there is very much the same.

Therefore, we developed social media primer training programs for clients to understand the basics of social media and its relation to the greater marketing communication landscape.

We helped clients design, develop, and maintain social media channels. We designed and deployed social media apps, Web apps (HTML5 apps that are mobile friendly), and native mobile apps for the iOS, Android, Blackberry, and Nokia. Our Internet Web development background since the commercial inception of the Internet, which was mostly in hand–coded HTML, PHP and Perl scripting, continue to be useful in today's social media and HTML5 world. Our knowledge management consulting background involving database–centric content management systems (CMS), also became extremely useful in helping clients with data–centric social media targeting.

At the end of the day, we as communication strategists have to keep pace and keep ahead of the curve of technologies, strategies, social and market preferences. We need to continue to evolve, adapt, learn, relearn, labor, and lead. It is what clients demand, and aspire to. It is our duty to fulfill them.

PR is hard work, and worth everything

Some people seem to imagine that public relations (PR) is glamorous and easy. They have no idea that PR is hard work, and often, many would move on to other things after some time. So why would people still work in PR?

Some of us have been PRSA (Public Relations Society of America) members for many years. PRSA is a great resource, and one of the regular publications we receive is TACTICS, which is an easy–to–read format with many succinct articles of the latest trends in PR.

In the July 2012 issue of TACTICS, Indra Gardiner wrote on the changing agency landscape, and her insights echoed what I thought as our own firm evolved from the early 1990s to today.

In the heydays of "high–tech" PR in the late 1990s, where many boutique PR agencies appeared on the scene, simply serving technology clients to communicate news and information to technology media. It was a period of exuberance. I recalled fondly many friends I made in the tech media, and eventually even started an editorial and research bureau, serving technology media with research, contributed articles, and even dabbled in TV and radio journalism. It was great fun. I thoroughly enjoyed that journey.

Then the dot–com era collapsed, and with it, many technology media folded as well, and many of my friends in technology journalism scattered to join other companies or fields. It was a sobering time of consolidation, and I returned to working in this firm, helping out with editorial, technology and training consulting again. It wasn't bad, but certainly required hard work all over again.

With every passing year, we began to notice that PR as a field that was traditionally pegged to mere media relations by many clients (and many clients still think PR is just media relations), began to widen and deepen as it should be.

PR today not only involves media relations, but very much provide holistic communication to all levels of stakeholders of a client company, including that of the fast–growing social media and mobile apps arena. Can we, as practitioners, stand still and remain in the yesteryears, with the skills and experience of yesteryears? Definitely not!

We had to evolve, quickly and aggressively, to nurture new skills and knowledge, stretching from social media to mobile app development. We continued to grow our expertise in our traditional offerings of human capital development, offering internal communication (training and development), as well as helping clients understand and develop their people better, which in turn, can translate to better service to their end–users, and better communication to all external stakeholders including the media, whether in print, broadcast, or online.

We have worked harder, even longer hours, learned like never before, and never felt more exhausted at times. Yet, while we comprehend the necessity of all these, we also recognize that there is an exhilaration that comes with equipping ourselves to be ready for the new world – one that changes by the minute. We live in exciting times that make incredible demands on us as practitioners. Are you ready?

The past, present, future of communication

There are three kinds of people. Some reminisce, some dream, and some live in the present. What do all these have to do with communication?

I have been in the communication and branding business as long as I have worked, and even before I started working. I was a young boy in junior school, and designed and developed magic tricks and brine shrimp kits for sale, designing my own packaging using my dad's manual typewriter, with my own illustrations, and then packaging the magic tricks and brine shrimp into products I sold to other kids in junior school. That was perhaps my first foray into business, and communication and branding along with it.

I love communication for what it represents, as a means to reach out to many people effectively and persuasively. I appreciate what it brings to those of us who love this field, to polish and hone our skills relentlessly, often without sufficient sleep – and yet enjoying it thoroughly with a knowing smile.

There are 3 kinds of people we see around today. Those who live in the past, those who live in the present, and those who "live in" the future.

Those who live in the past often remember all the details of their past, whether it be glorious or sad. The trouble is that one who lives in the past will find it hard to move forward. Those who had beautiful memories of a pampered and privileged past, may invariably shrink from the present simply because they believe their best times are gone. Those who had sad or traumatic memories may be scarred and are not healed sufficiently to move forward to live in the present, which may well be better than the terrible past.

For example, let's say Tom was the best cello player in the school orchestra during his teens, but gave up on his musical inclinations to pursue a business degree and is now an account executive in a design studio. He has altered his path in life, perhaps for rational reasons. Would Tom be happier if he accepts his portion in life now and be contented? Or would Tom be happier if he lets go of his current job and rekindle his musical talents, foregoing material comforts perhaps? It is a choice Tom has to make.

Those who dream about the future often may become idealistic, if their everyday actions do not form the foundation to build towards the future they dream about.

Let's say John is currently working as an engineer in a factory, but he really wanted to be a chef. Should John continue to daydream, or should he begin to study options to work towards becoming a chef, perhaps by attending night school or apprenticing in a small restaurant? It is also a choice John has to make to turn empty chatter and dreams into a reality.

There are those who live in and for the present. This does not mean these people have no memories or choose not to bother with their past. Many people have happy or sad experiences in life, but they adapt to them and move on. They do not become complacent based on past achievements, but make every day forward count with new or renewed effort, maintaining pace and discipline, and loving every moment. They do not neglect to understand what could happen in the future, but are realistic in making plans, and carrying out such plans towards the future, one day at a time.

This brings us to the field of communication. I was watching Season Three of Mad Men, an award–winning TV series about the world of advertising. In one of the episodes, the lead character reminded us that communicating effectively with the public cannot be static and stagnant, or obsessive. Fiction often mimics life, and we can easily find the realities we live as communicators when we watch the TV series.

For example, when a client insists that we, the specialists, communicate to the public a message that we know is simply not going to fly, and may turn against the client's company, we should be upfront with the client. The client is not always right, and we are the specialists.

It is akin to instructing a surgeon how to operate on you, when you should relinquish everything to the surgeon and trust in his expertise. Otherwise, don't engage a surgeon.

In such a scenario, the client also needs to understand that public relations does not mean saying meaningless words hoping to comfort an angry mob.

True communication is about maintaining engagement and conversation with the public, in a rational and meaningful way.

Imagine you are at a cocktail party. You can choose to chat with certain people, or you can stay silent and blissfully watch people go by while enjoying your drink.

When you choose certain people to chat with, not every subject that pops up will hold your interest. You can switch subjects, or you can switch conversation partners. It is that simple, and it applies to communication. How?

Public relations is merely a facet of holistic communications. At the same time, internal communication is just as important, if not more so.

We help clients communicate corporate programs and ideas to their own employees, through internal human resource development (HRD) programs. We also help clients with crisis prevention and crisis recovery development programs, helping them prepare for any eventuality with assurance, fortitude, stability, honesty, and grace. We also help clients examine all the communication tactics available today and the future, whether it be mainstream advertising, direct marketing, social media, public and trade events, mobile apps, outdoor advertising, any established or emerging communication means – to get the message across. It is our duty to present all sensible options to clients, just as a surgeon has the duty to present all sensible options to help clients make the wisest decision.

Financially committed and enlightened clients recognize the need for holistic communications, and why and how it will help their brands, their public reputation, and their returns on investments (ROI).

The cost, complexity and maintenance of PR tools

I remember fondly, the first time I wrote a news release and sent it off in a printed media kit. I presented the media kit to each of the journalists I spoke with, and many of them became friends. That was in the early nineties. Every media event I organized when I was a marketing manager, and attended in later years as a journalist, the printed news release was the norm. Eventually, the printed news release transformed into email releases and RSS (really simple syndication) news feeds.

Today, the landscape for news releases is no longer simple, and textual news releases are fast becoming just a small facet of news information for journalists and the public alike. What are some of these vehicles of communication?

For communication practitioners and marketers, there are now many diverse tactical approaches to maintaining and building your brand and reputation.

The simplest is still the news release. There are also tactical vehicles such as white papers and articles, that we can submit to relevant media for repurposing or as background material. Complementing news releases and papers is the digital media kit, or online media kit. A digital media kit provides a collation of news releases, backgrounder information, white papers, research articles, images (photographs and illustrations), and maybe removable media such as CD–ROMs or USB storage, where all the news materials can be retrieved by the journalists easily.

The online media kit takes all these materials and are hosted on a server, and journalists simply visit the website to retrieve all the news materials. For places where bandwidth is developed and stable, the online media kit is the best option to reduce material wastage, while providing the marketers and practitioners the possibility of analytics whenever journalists download specific news information.

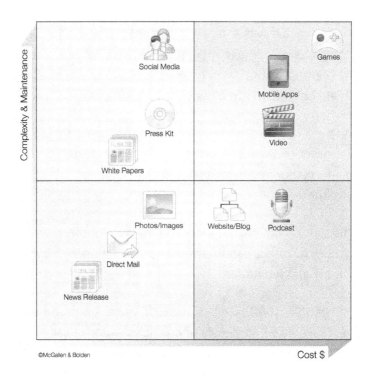

©McGallen & Bolden

Cost $

Images are paramount in good storytelling. Journalists often demand high quality images that fit their editorial guidelines. Moving up the complexity and cost ladder are audio and video, which will empower your brand much more, as more people turn to online video for news and reference, on desktops, tablets, and even smartphones.

Social media is also a channel to tap on, from the consumer and promotions–driven platforms to the vertical business and career–centric social media platforms. There are specific ways to communicate news information for each social media platform.

Increasingly, there is a mobilization of news and content, as more people turn to news on their smartphones and tablets rather than traditional media channels. Analysts observe the trend that eventually, the majority of news users will read and view news information on mobile devices, and the majority of users will view video news rather than read textual news. It is a reality we as practitioners must come to terms with and adapt to these changes quickly and effectively.

If we take the mass transit to work in the mornings, it is easy to see many younger people on their smartphones and tablets, not just listening to music or watching videos, but playing games. The new generation is adept at playing digital games, and it is a platform that can be leveraged by marketers and communication practitioners as well.

Some companies are "gamifying" their corporate content to create entertaining news and content that engages users, rather than present cold, dead, and boring facts. Integrating a mobile and "gamified" strategy requires a high–maintenance blog, microsite or website, with content that are tightly intertwined with mobile apps (native, hybrid, or HTML5 Web apps) and other social and online games. It is the most complex platform, but presents very transformational and engaging content.

Measuring PR effectiveness

One of the most disputed measurements in public relations was "Advertising Value Equivalency" (AVE), which simplistically takes the advertising cost of a particular media and equate it to an "equivalency" in advocacy and reputation. This approach became outdated due to the following:

1. Lack the value of credibility.

2. Wrongly treats placement simply as "paid advertising."

3. Does not address quality of content relative to tone and size.

4. Does not address readership or audience reach.

5. Does not compare fairly to circulation versus population and GDP (PPP) per capita, consumer spending percentage, relative to other related media, etc.

6. Does not factor in the heterogeneity of nations relative to media, language, and outreach.

How, then, can public relations measurement be more realistic and more equitable to clients, agencies, media, and cross–border national comparisons?

Public relations campaigns are often cross–border and marketers are held accountable for the effectiveness of the campaigns in each nation they deploy them in. Yet, each nation presents different variables such as population, GDP (which has a relative value to consumer spending), percentage of consumer spending by GDP, total number of equivalent media in that nation, circulation of specific media, campaign length, and so on.

"Advertising value equivalence" (AVE) is a rudimentary and inaccurate measurement of public relations effectiveness that still has some use, but should be calculated in conjunction with all the variables together. The derivative value is not a dollar value, but a fairer indicator of national public relations effectiveness by campaign. A fair public relations effectiveness can be measured against these following factors:

1. Media cost.

2. Circulation or audience.

3. Tone of coverage (positive, negative, or neutral).

4. Size of mention (feature, quote, or name mention).

5. GDP PPP per capita and consumer spending against population.

6. Number of equivalent media (e.g. 1 English coverage in a newspaper against a total of 10 similar newspapers).

7. Length of campaign.

8. Campaign cost.

9. Analytics of target market effects.

Before you get mired in controversial and unequal measurements of "apples and oranges" in your campaigns in the future, perhaps it is time to create a better measurement system to discern just how effective your regional, national, or global campaigns are, with a fuller set of indicators. It will be more work, but certainly the results would make more analytical and financial sense to the top executives.

Less static, more moving sights and sounds

Public relations and communication are at the crossroads for many practitioners, with the avalanche of social media and mobile apps beating down conventional communication channels for a slice of the pie, if not the whole pie sometimes. What can practitioners do?

We can sit on the fence and hope to sit out the game until the dust settles; or we can dive head in with preparation, expertise, and a smile.

I was reading the respected industry magazine "Campaign" and came across an advertisement which quoted the networking giant Cisco (2009), that by 2013, 90% of all Web traffic will be video content. This prediction lends anxiety and excitement at the same time.

I believe the textual news release and other written communication collaterals can still have some relevance, even as more people are turning to video content. YouTube and Vimeo are some of the most turned-to information and entertainment sources today, with a multitude of other video hosting platforms coming to the forefront, contesting for the same audiences for attention.

A textual news release may still reach a journalist, but if a textual news release comes with associated video content and other downloaded materials, coupled with analytics, it will likely produce more coverage while giving an additional means to engage new audiences.

In the 1990s, we were amongst the first to self–produce, in–house, multimedia media kits for high–tech clients. Those were the days of 3.5–inch floppy disks, and we were able to compress and fit Macromedia Director files down through heavy graphics optimization into the floppies. It was hard work, but tremendously rewarding as the media were impressed with interactive presentations with the news materials.

The floppy disk has become a figment of computing history, replaced by DVD and USB drives, and then, the cloud. Still, the need to impress and engage the media through interactive media releases and media kits is stronger than ever before.

Today, we need to prioritize with video interviews (or video news releases/VNRs), complete with annotations and click–through links to Web content and social media channels, uploaded to dedicated websites, micro–sites, or social media channels, because even audio podcasts have fallen in demand.

We need to create original and innovative news angles and pitches to demonstrate the importance of client products and services. We can no longer afford to simply imagine the journalists would pick up any news release we send over. We respect our colleagues in the media, and know that their time is precious, their objectives are to communicate news (and not sales pitches) to their audiences and readers, with as much engagement as we possibly can imagine or create. The job of the public relations practitioner is more challenging than ever before, and yet, what fun! Lights, camera, action!

The transitioning tech media

With a tinge of sadness, we have watched the technology media scene transform and decay.

In the 1990s, I was a contributing writer for technology media, locally and internationally. It was an exciting time where the pace of development in the Internet arena accelerated beyond our imagination, and everything with the word "Internet" in its soul, seemed to take off, got noticed, and attracted investments. Besides consulting and speaking professionally, I got into the tech circuit too, and managed to develop Web properties and software in Perl, PHP and Java.

Then by 2000, the dot–com world came tumbling down suddenly, and one by one the hot Internet startups and emerging companies dropped off the radar, and with them, some technology media as well. My gigs as a contributing editor for some great technology magazines as well as a foreign broadcast correspondent for an American TV channel ceased around then, as those media transitioned and some closed.

Fortunately, I was still speaking and consulting professionally. But the romance with technology journalism drew to a lamenting close.

I still harbor thoughts of working with technology media again, but the landscape in this locale is decidedly different. There aren't that many opportunities for old hats like me anymore, with many of my former peers now in academia, or like me, in public relations or marketing. Some have quit the media and communication fields altogether, and have gone on to other unrelated areas.

For some technology companies, especially those with consumer technology products that reach out to the mass market, there are still consumer technology media and general lifestyle media, as well as the spectrum of mainstream media such as dailies, weeklies, radio, and TV.

There are also emerging online media that are technology–centric, and lifestyle bloggers who write about consumer technology. For enterprise technology companies, the options for media coverage are far less. Even as some clients might imagine every enterprise technology newsworthy for broadsheets, TV and radio, the reality is that such news are niche and targeted, and have no relevance to the generic public. Clients need to understand that niche and targeted news meant for a small audience, will require vehicles that specifically call out to these small audience groups.

For example, there are trade journals, vertical trade magazines, online trade media, trade associations' internal publications and websites, and so on.

There are many ways to approach technology publicity today. We can reach out to specific audiences directly through carefully developed micro–sites featuring quality textual and video content, and propagate to social media platforms.

Would the technology media become vibrant and expansive again? I hope so. Until then, we expand our options creatively.

How hands–on are your communication consultants?

Communication firms large and small are streamlining their operations to restructure roles of their staffers, to move with the changing needs of clients and the new media horizon.

In the old days, when I briefly flirted with the advertising industry as a production manager and account executive, the advertising agency of that era had strict hierarchies – general management, account management, creatives, production, media, and so on. Lateral movements were out of the question then. Creatives remain as creatives, account executives (or "suits") remain so as well, until they reach the top (or end) of their careers.

Today, some communication firms are already changing how they are run. Many have seen just how brutal the market forces are, how fierce the onslaught of the economic slowdown (and more storms are coming), and how few good and committed talents are available. Instead of highly hierarchical setups, many firms, even larger ones, are beginning to flatten their hierarchies, and reducing the ranks of generalists in their folds.

After all, clients do not like to talk to mere "suits," who then have to return to their offices to brief their creative and media teams, with liberal margins of translation errors in between. While some people, even young graduates, are hoping to be "suits" and hope to rise up the ranks to helm such firm, the trend is not moving in their wishful direction.

These days, everyone has to rise up and be counted, be ready to serve the firm's interests and the client's interests, with specialized and needed skills. There is no more reason for errors of translation between what the client wants, and how and what the firm is going to do. The client expects whoever talking to have the technical and creative expertise to pen down proper plans and strategies moving forward – thereby reducing errors, reducing extraneous costs, and reducing wasted time of meaningless production and creative meetings.

This is true for advertising agencies as it is for other communication firms such as public relations (PR) and new media firms, and is applicable to just about any industry.

We have always been compelled to either led the curve, or was in pace with emerging developments, simply as a means of survival in a fierce marketplace. As a small firm, there is little hierarchy because there is no reason or budget to. Everyone has to develop specific skill sets that would serve the needs of the media and the clients, and we help each other in plans and programs that would translate to successes for clients.

For example, we were the first in our area to develop floppy–disk interactive media kits with animations, digital media, and so on, in the mid–1990s even before the Internet became commercially available. We developed a short film for a high–tech client with a storyline, even before the dot–com era ended. We have kept pace with technology developments, designing and developing our own media and production systems. We have set up online media newsrooms for clients, and now also develop online video content, e–commerce, social media, and other new media content for clients, helping our clients keep pace with the communication needs of the current generation.

One practice area that we have had long experience with are video news releases (VNRs). We have done field work in operating video cameras and HD DSLR cameras, with handheld rigs and stabilizers, audio systems, chromakey (blue–screen), animation, and desktop video editing (we used the AVID NLEs as far back as the nineties). These developmental work involved hard work, and compels us to keep learning, keep trying, keep doing. Long hours, sweat and tears are the daily grind.

Time waits for no one, and the communication environment is evolving very fast, sometimes faster than we'd like. The days of merely writing news releases and sending media kits by postal mail to the media are long over. The media scene itself has transformed a great deal, with the need to develop custom owned media properties for clients to deepen the outreach and engagement with the public, rather than only through traditional mainstream media alone.

As a owner or manager of a company, you may increasingly find that you expect your communication consultant to actually be the person doing the hard work, coming out with the new ideas, and keeping track of the campaign developments.

And you are 100% right in your expectations. Your communication firm should lead your needs, and know about all the communication technologies and applications firsthand with field experience, and alleviate your burdens to simply help you become more successful.

Do you have a communications fire drill?

All too often, we see some companies reacting (sometimes badly) to crises with last minute communication plans and panicky spokespersons. Since no company can predict or prevent potential crises, what needs to be done?

When we talk about crisis communications, there must first be a crisis preparedness program in place within the company that all stakeholders are ready for.

Just as office buildings often conduct fire drills regularly, a company needs a communications fire drill in place.

What makes a good crisis communications program?

1. Ensure there is a program of crisis prevention in place. Managers and front-liners of all departments of a company should keep their ears to the ground, and understand the pulse of the marketplace. There should be a culture of encouraging comments and  advice from all employees within the company. All these constructive comments should be consolidated into a frequently asked questions (FAQ) database that anyone can read and contribute to. Make the FAQ database similar to a corporate wiki, where authenticated contributors can all edit and add to the knowledge–base.

2. Implement a crisis communications program. All stakeholders should be educated on what this program is, and what would ignite this program. For example, what would be a crisis be, and what would a non–critical event be? The program can also highlight who should an employee turn to in a crisis? Who can be a spokesperson? Who would be involved parties to provide educated and truthful answers?

3. All employees need to be actively engaged in scheduled and unscheduled communications fire drills, so that any employee on board should be as ready as the top executives. In such drills, simulated crises can be set up so that all stakeholders know what needs to be done, and how to do it. Unscheduled drills will be useful to ensure that employees are prepared for any eventuality. The reason front–liners are just as important as the top executives (often designated spokespersons) is that the media may interview your front–lines, and without a proper crisis communications program, your front–liners will be caught embarrassingly off guard.

4. Remember that your public relations (PR) agency is your strategic partner in helping you define, design, and deploy such a crisis communications program. It is a holistic program that addresses external communications when a crisis occurs, and importantly, provides an educational program that helps all your employees become acutely aware of how best to handle a crisis even before it occurs.

A crisis cannot be predicted, much as natural calamities cannot be. However, being prepared for all possible eventualities, is critical. Don't be caught off guard, be prepared.

3 tips of making niche news useful to more people

Have you heard clients banging on the table wanting front–page news or prominent mention? What are the best ways of communicating good counsel to them?

One of the disconnects between some clients and their PR counselors has to be just what public relations is. To some, public relations is mistakenly seen as a cheaper way of "advertising."

To these clients, they would often say, "Can you guarantee the placement of my product launch in all the daily newspapers?" We can tell them, "Yes, we can guarantee the placement of your product news in all the daily newspapers. The special projects teams of the newspapers can help you with a special advertorial, a paid space, that will be able to position your new product in the exact messaging that you prefer. We can help craft and edit the messaging to your preference. The budget for such advertorials will be $XYZ."

Some clients may believe ANYTHING they say or want to say is newsworthy, as newsworthy as national elections, major scandals, global economic slowdowns, major natural disasters, major sporting news, or news of similar magnitude affecting many. Public relations implies that news has to serve the public at large, be important enough for the masses, and serve public interest. A commercial launch of a niche product would = never qualify as news that serve the public at large and be important for the masses. Being a commercial product launch with an agenda of selling the products for a profit would not be serving public interest either.

Therefore, as counselors, we have to be honest with clients, and educate them on just what newsworthy stories can be, and how best to communicate commercial or niche products and their launches.

There are many means to communicate such products and launches, especially in the expanded communication platforms such as social media even as some mainstream communication channels are diminishing. Beyond tapping on new methods of communication, such as using social media, setting up micro–sites and RSS feeds, and developing custom mobile and Web apps, we can also advise clients to look at the messaging itself.

Since a commercial product launch would not qualify as "breaking news," how do we refine the messaging of such a launch to make it relevant to as many people as possible?

Without going into the specifics necessary to dissect specific products and how they can be launched, let us instead think of 3 succinct ways to describe how to make a commercial news useful to the media.

1. Is there something **thought–provoking** in our messaging of the product and the launch? Are there pointed questions that we can ask upfront, to describe a pressing need, or a need that most people never thought existed?

2. What kind of **deep insights** can we provide in our product messaging, whether it be analyses of global, regional or local trends, technological movements, usability studies, etc?

These insights would not come easy, and demand research and statistics, but will be seen as useful by the media.

3. How do we **position** the product as useful to as many people at the same time? This again demands research into the product. A product may serve the direct needs of a small group of administrators but may have great repercussions on the greater population of a corporation.

Therefore, rather than simply centering on the product specifications and features, we examine how the product would impact the people who manage or administer such products, and how the product can affect the greater communities of people within a corporation (or even beyond).

Therefore, rather than zoom in on individual customers who may adopt the product, consider the greater influence of such products to the greater population.

Using the example of a network security product, which is traditionally seen as a niche and enterprise product, we can look beyond the obvious. Security is not just something network administrators worry about, but has repercussions on the entire corporation and its user base, and also its interaction with its stakeholders – its customers, shareholders, partners, the public population, and so on.

Explore as many possible communication channels as possible, taking into account the mainstream media, the trade media, the social channels, and even the Web and mobile platforms.

It is a rapidly evolving world and communication is evolving just as rapidly. Clients and public relations counselors have to adapt to this new paradigm, together, and fast.

More important for clients, what are the products they are pitching to the public, and how can these products influence the greater population with relevance?

We as counselors are responsible for being honest with our clients as much as we have to do sufficient research, and demand our clients do that too, to bring the most relevant information to reach out to as many communities as possible.

5 critical observations of the future of public relations

Public Relations (PR) has gone through evolutionary and even revolutionary changes from the nineties.

Before the emergence of social media, online video, online newsrooms, and citizen journalism, it seemed many organizations and practitioners narrowed public relations to merely media relations and measured public relations only as a factor of the antiquated "advertising value equivalence" (AVE).

Today, public relations has gone much further. Here are 5 important things to consider.

1. **Be holistic**. Public relations is one facet of corporate communication but not the end–all and be–all. Public relations exists as a subset of a holistic and effective corporate communication program, alongside internal communication, advertising, events, direct marketing, and so on. Plan and think holistic.

2. **Media Relations is a mere subset of public relations**. We need to cater to the entire spectrum of stakeholders, that would include the media, but also institutions, customers, prospects, and the public. The idea of "word–of–mouth" advertising is not new, and proven to be effective. We need to engage every stakeholder possible, to maximize the client's brand, its products and services, and its reputation.

3. **Public relations is the summation of facts and storytelling**. Public relations is not a direct sales tool, and must be set

aside as a serious, respectable, credible information source that can be relied upon by the media and other stakeholders alike. Therefore, facts (information that can be proven to be true) must be present in news information and collaterals. At the same time, news information must not be boring. The best way to persuade through credible public relations is not a "sell, sell, sell" approach, but through the presentation of facts with a good case story as the frontrunner. A story well and truthfully told will get you the greatest mileage.

4. **Think social, mobile, and visual**. Public relations is not just about a textual news release sent to hundreds of journalists. Today, you have to present news to the social media and the mobile platforms, as these become increasingly news and information sources many people rely on (as secondary sources, and sometimes even as primary sources). At the same time, your news must soar beyond the printed page, and jump off the screen as sounds, pictures, and video. At the same time, more people read news off their smartphones and tablets. You need to reach out to the mobile audience.

5. **Own your news**. Public relations is no longer the ceding of content to the mainstream media and hope you get mileage and coverage. You need to own your news. An online newsroom with online video, podcasts, and images, is a must–have today, as you extend and expand your media outreach by owning your content that we develop and deliver for you, as well as reaching out to traditional mainstream media. Many multinational corporations and emerging ones have empowered themselves with their own news properties. Shouldn't you?

Pottery and spokespersons

If you have an important task, such as needing a spokesperson to evangelize your product, or a salesperson to close a big sale, or a surgeon to operate on a life–threatening ailment, who would you choose?

Unfortunately, it gets harder to discern if someone actually has the field–proven, battle–tested skills and knowledge you need to get a job done. There are many graduates who may have the confidence to persuade you that they can do the job well (and they may). The crux is if there is something important and is hanging in the balance, can things be left to mere chance?

We were at the Yingge District of New Taipei, Taiwan, which is known for its pottery. We wanted to see the pottery museum and to try our hands at making pottery. I have been an art club president during high school, and was good at pottery. I figured it would be easy to pick up pottery again, at least for fun.

When we sat down to knead the moist clay, I suddenly realized how foreign the clay appeared to me. The feeling of the clay in my hands was alien and I took more time than I liked to attempt to sculpt the clay. My early confidence vanished, and humility and genuine effort began to set in. I was able to finish one piece of work at the end of the session.

Likewise in our roles, having done something before may embolden us to imagine that we are capable of finishing particular jobs, and we may even have the false confidence to imagine we can get these jobs done faster than reality. For the young, they too may imagine that merely graduating from a college means that they can easily get a job done.

In the field of communication, a great spokesperson takes laborious pains to practice their presentations until it is honed to an art. I have been speaking on stage professionally, and from field experience, my peers and I often prepare, refine, and tweak our messages and presentations, until only the essence remains. The Chinese have a saying, "a minute on stage is backed by a decade of hard work and practice." How true! So, we need to help our clients practice their delivery often.

Likewise, the best salespersons hone their message, their knowledge of the products, their presentations, their manner of delivery, and how they interact with people through many failures and rejections, before they become top of their trade.

For trade professionals, whether surgeons, craftsmen, engineers, architects, lawyers, and so on, the scenario is the same – a great deal of time is spent on continuous learning and practice, where frequent failures are diagnosed and digested.

Therefore, it is important to inculcate in our teams the importance of continuous learning and practice. You fail once, you get up and continue learning and doing. Young or old alike, the same rules apply. Just because someone has done it before does not mean that he is as good today.

What's more, the world is changing so fast that the knowledge and skills acquired before, may already be obsolete the moment we are ready to tackle the next challenge. For the spokespersons, salespeople, advocates and service professionals, keep practicing, keep learning.

Depth of field and the publicity "home run"

If you are a serious photographer, you would be familiar with shallow depth of field (DOF).

Images with shallow DOF are more dramatic, and lead us to focus on specific things. What does shallow DOF have to do with publicity and branding?

Our human eyes are unlike zoom lenses on video and still cameras. Our human eyes retain sharp focus on all objects within their sights. Our brains do all the superlative processing to bring our sights and focus to specific people or objects, rather than our eyes.

Therefore, when you try to look around you, you will notice that you can't blur out the background when you are looking at an object in the foreground. Any "blurring of the background" is perceptual, as your brain shuts out the background. The camera is very different. With zoom lenses, you can zoom in and out of a visual scene easily, without moving closer or away from the scene (unlike our eyes).

If you have tried photography, you would notice an "f–stop" number range on a camera lens. The lower the f–stop number, the more expensive the lens may be. For example, if you have a 50 mm lens with an f–stop of 3.5 (or f/3.5), it will be much cheaper compared to a 50 mm lens with f/1.2. The lower the f–stop, the wider the aperture can be open, allowing more light in, and are more capable of creating images with shallower DOF. Lenses with shallow DOF can blur out the background while retaining sharpness for foreground objects, and such lenses are often used for portraiture, fashion, advertising, and macro photography.

Seamus Phan

What has shallow DOF lenses got to do with publicity? Plenty.

In many companies, it is relatively challenging to maintain objectivity when looking at our own products and services. We are immersed and entrenched in our own products and services, and invariably, affected by our own unfiltered view of our entire product or service landscape, especially in relation to the rest of the world or marketplace out there.

Conversely, imagine the publicity consultant as your special purpose lens, the lens with the shallow DOF, capable of zooming into to specific products and services, and helping you bring focus to them to the world.

A good publicity consultant not only brings expertise and experience to the table, but can also help you filter out the background noise of your competition, and the background noise of your other products and services, and bring laser–sharp focus to just the product or service you want to focus on for the moment. Why is this important?

When approaching the media or the consumers, all too often we lose sight of how important focused messaging can be. We may inadvertently cloud our messaging, hoping to bring the media and the consumers' attention to everything we sell. Since the human attention span is limited, we need to zoom in and focus on just one product or service, with a refined message that would pitch a home run to the media, and to the consumers.

The next time you are carried away with trying to pitch a spectrum of fantastic products and services under your stable, bring in a good publicity consultant.

The consultant would be your filter to the world, the zoom lens with the shallow depth of field, to help bring a single product or service, with a solid pitch, to the world. Each product or service will enjoy its exposure to the world, one campaign at a time.

Amidst the noise out there, it may just be the home run you seek.

dot zen 2.0

Social Media & the Web

3 tips of website optimization for marketing campaigns

Here's a typical scenario. A consumer products company engaged an interactive media agency to design a marketing campaign website for consumer engagement.

While the site looks flashy, it ran into many usability problems. How do you design a website for marketing that just works? What went wrong with that website's usability in this scenario?

1. The site may rely on the current version of Flash, which some users may not have and needed to download. Not many consumers are willing to have to download an updated plugin just to view a website.

2. The site may have been developed in a manner that was not the most optimized, resulting in hogging available bandwidth and some users would report that they could not interact with the website properly. The result? The users gave up.

An effective website or microsite for marketing campaigns needs to embrace the following:

1. **Open standards such as HTML5**. The late Mr Steve Jobs was visionary to know that open standards empower both end–users and developers for the most collaborative application environment that is good for the whole ecosystem. Therefore, when you are thinking of a microsite or website for marketing campaigns, developing in HTML5 means that the content can easily be targeted for the desktop Web environment, as well as most modern smartphones,

especially those that don't run Flash. It is important to get a Web and mobile app developer who understands HTML5 and other open standards so that your marketing campaigns can reach out to the widest audience possible without shutting many others. Adobe announced it will cease development for mobile versions of Flash and focus on their AIR platform instead*. This has repercussions for developers trying to target multiple platforms. Developing for HTML5 as a primary platform makes sense for small and larger developers alike.

2. **Optimize the multimedia content**. Videos and audio content are important in engaging for end–users. However, dumping large bandwidth–hogging multimedia content onto the users' computers or smartphones, will only drive them away rather than engage them. After all, not everyone has a fiber optic network to tap on. Get an expert to help you optimize the multimedia down to palatable sizes. There is always a decent compromise on rich audiovisual content and bandwidth. There are also many different audio and video formats that may work on some desktop and mobile platforms, and not on others. Get a developer who is not just someone who converts audio and video for the websites, but someone who knows audio and video production and post–production.

3. **Interactivity**. Websites for marketing campaigns should be inherently interactive. Again, the method to deliver interactivity should rely on open standards, and perhaps even reusable code for future campaigns. Encasing everything into proprietary formats may be good for developers trying to secure their development, but it is challenging for end–user clients to manage in a rapidly changing world. Using an open standard such as HTML5 and

languages such as PHP for interactivity, will mean that should you need to hand off the project to another developer for some good reason, there is a higher chance for your project to enjoy continuity in the future.

Marketing campaigns should be fast–to–market, easily adapted and changed for market and consumer demands, and can retain relevance for a technological landscape that keeps evolving. The technological means to get your campaigns out there, should not be an impediment to your customers, nor to you.

* http://www.infoworld.com/d/the–industry–
standard/adobe–ends–mobile–flash–player–
reveals–enterprise–pullback–178474

The long and short form of content targeting

Content is key. It still is. The need for useful information is still there, although readers are increasingly bombarded with both textual and audiovisual content today.

While the attention span of some readers may be short and require short–form writing, there are other readers who desire long–form writing. What should we do? Do both.

Mainstream newspapers and magazines have traditionally been long–form stalwarts, with lengthy features that are written with flair and authority, populated by fact–checked background information and facts.

Today, the content in newspapers has become more succinct, catering to the fast–moving contemporary lifestyles.

Magazines on the other hand, at least the thriving big names, have stuck to the long–form writing that readers are used to and still demand.

Mainstream newspapers and magazines have also gone online and mobile, with abstracts and specially condensed versions of their articles catering to online and mobile users.

The surge in social media platforms such as Twitter, LinkedIn and Facebook, have also created a whole new genre of short–form writing, whether from journalists, bloggers or even individuals alike.

Today, everyone with a cell phone, a tablet, or a computer, can claim to be a writer of some kind. Everyone seems to at least have a small, and sometimes larger readership. The nature of media has shifted its gravity from mainstream big names, to a whole new ecosystem that is enlivened by blogs, emerging online media, tweets and short posts.

No two readers are alike, and that certainly creates a new level of complexity and more work for the information publisher. Some like writings short, some like them long and elaborate.

Therefore, while we acknowledge content is key, we need to create content that target readers with different preferences in brevity and length. It is possible.

The trick is to have writers target the long–form articles first, and then have someone condense the articles down to target short–form platforms such as blogs and mobile apps.

One size does not fit all, especially in the scenario of large multinational corporations with cross–border brands. More work is demanded of the information publisher and his team, and the time is now.

4 key questions to ask about social media marketing

Social media is all the rage, perhaps the flavor of the moment. At every café, every turn of the corner, in college, on the bus, practically anywhere, you can find someone on social media, tapping away on their smartphone or a tablet.

For companies large and small, most would have dabbled in social media first as an experiment, and then progressively integrate the experiment into their overall marketing program. Some may have given up along the way, relegating the medium to a fearful and failed experiment.

However, beyond the occasional and ad hoc experiment with social media, companies have to analyze social media and see how the tool can become not just a tactical part of the marketing program, but have a strategic and creative direction as well. Ask yourself a few questions.

1. **What kind of social media tools will you use**? Do you have a content–driven Web property that can integrate well with the social media tools you choose? Have you made provisions for emerging and future social media tools that may perform the same way, only better; or tools that will revolutionize the functionality of social media in new ways?

2. **Who on your team can manage the social media marketing tools**? If there is no one, what kind of individuals should you look for? If you have identified potential candidates within the company, do they already have the prerequisite skills and

knowledge? If not, how do you plan to help them get up to speed and get productive?

3. **Have you analyzed how social media as a marketing tool complement your traditional marketing tools and tactics?** How would you integrate these social media tools with print, broadcast and other online platforms? What kind of measurements are you looking at?

4. **Have you identified a strategic program** consisting of workflow, content frameworks, creative delivery, audience engagement, timeline, etc? If so, document it well in a collaborative platform so that your team's stakeholders can all collaborate in a networked environment to track execution, deadlines, programs, stakeholders, measurements, etc. Think corporate wiki as a collaborative platform to track the program.

It seems fun to test the waters of social media platforms and tools for a while. After the initial hype and euphoria, social media is but a tool and a single slice of the greater holistic marketing program. It is a tactical approach, and part of the arsenal of marketing tools we use for specific outreach and specific campaigns. It should not be an orphaned experiment.

3 considerations for quality Web, social and mobile content

Despite what you may have heard, a successful Web and social media presence is still about having quality content that people want to know about. Focus on content, and less on tricks.

When we started consulting for multinational corporations and government agencies when Internet became commercially available in the nineties, one of the first things we did and continued to focus on was content. The earliest websites we created were content–rich, rather than following on the trail of fancy animations and superfluous designs. We created one of the pioneering content portals (Global Asia) way back in 1996, featuring interesting sights and sounds in our region, as well as websites we designed for clients in government, industry, retail, electronics, and fashion.

The rules of engagement on the Web remains fundamentally the same today, albeit having been through some detours and distractions along the way.

For example, just some years ago, I received many spam emails purporting to improve our search engine optimization (SEO) through some esoteric means, for a fee. I have been an Internet programmer, developer and designer since 1996, and I am deeply familiar with SEO and all the techniques they peddled.

Those techniques might have worked before, but search engines these days have much more sophisticated techniques of indexing websites and content, as well as rejecting junk and spam content just as readily. Stuffing pages with keywords, links, and meta tags, have become anywhere from meaningless to taboo. The reality is that search engines have gotten much smarter than many marketers may have you believe. The crux is down to if you have good and readable content or not.

A recent article by Michael Mothner is a great reminder.

Let's also remember that websites are not much different from social networking sites. Social network properties are also content–driven, just like quality websites are. Some companies have social media properties only populated with product advertisements, with little else to engage their users.

Worse, some marketers or consultants may persuade clients that investments can be measured in terms of "likes," which has very little meaning. Truthfully, some users "like" a social media page simply to criticize negatively, which is ironical to the word "like." It is no wonder that many companies report poor social media investments based on erroneous analytics.

Social media properties are not advertisement billboards, but are more akin to realtime forums where users and owners can interact equitably with each other, exchanging and sharing together collegially.

Stephanie Chandler wrote an enlightening and timely reminder, that we must always blog regularly on our social media properties. A social media presence is just like your website – it should not be a tomb of cold, dead information, but lively and continually updated forums of excitement.

Taking the Web and social media a step further, and we have the mobile evolution.

Increasingly, more users reach out to content on the mobile device, whether a smartphone or a tablet. With 3G and now 4G reaching out to many places, it becomes easier to retrieve and read content on a smartphone or an untethered tablet.

Therefore, by extending our outreach to the mobile platform with HTML5 or native apps, we need to think of the mobile app as a content extension platform, rather than a billboard or advertisement. The same logic and advice applies.

One of the key stumbling blocks some clients face with the Web, social media, and mobile apps, is that they find it difficult to blog and create quality content.

1. **Get a good content manager** who has the focus of an editor, the words of a journalist, the perspective of a researcher, the vision and charisma of a good leader. Then get this person to assemble a team (either in–house, or outsourced), to run the holistic Web, social media and mobile platform as a content–centric environment.

2. **Quality content** must engage your users. Therefore, take some liberties at creating interesting topics and content that would engage users to discuss and occasionally debate about (in a positive way, and moderated). Do not be trapped or caged by boring corporate–speak that nobody (but your bosses) want to read about. Get innovative, get creative, get expressive.

3. **Invest wisely and boldly**. A good technology–centric outreach is no longer a long body of text, but is succinct on words, and rich in interactive media. You need to be enlightened to invest in creating video content and interactive games, integrating them together to target the Web, social media, and mobile platforms. Invest little and you end up with hopeless properties that are no different from a printed brochure. There is a cost that comes with quality.

The world is overloaded with information, especially unprocessed information that bombards our senses relentlessly. Yet, in the mountains of it all, good content that engages users will always stand out at the top of the heap, shared by many, and profitable when done right.

Organic reach and media ownership

When Facebook became available to corporations in the use of "fan pages", we designed and developed corporate training primer programs for our clients, to provide the basic level of competency for our clients and their marketers.

Not long after, we refined the training primer to include other platforms that became available or relevant to corporations. It became apparent that the training programs had to be tweaked often, because of the fluidity of social networks, their technologies and policies. Such frequent changes invariably affect our organic outreach to our customers using such platforms. How can we manage and control our content and outreach on such platforms and beyond?

The social network platforms have increasingly become a content and advertising platform for many, especially because many are enticed by the millions of users who use such platforms, whether infrequently or frequently.

Social networks can be immediately fun, social, adventurous, and at the same time, distracting and time–wasting, depending on what you do, and how they affect others.

Marketers are trapped in a sense that they cannot ignore social networks in a holistic marketing strategy, and sometimes find it hard to explain it away even if social networks may not really make sense in the constraints of their organizations.

Social networks are also ever–changing, whether with back–end technologies, user interfaces (UIs), the plugins and widgets, analytics, and even algorithms, all making the development and deployment of social network marketing complex and high–maintenance for marketers.

Let us as business owners and executives first empathize that some social networks are set up as businesses and not charities or open source initiatives, with stakeholders requiring decent returns on investment, just as ours do.

Therefore, it is not unimaginable that social networks must find ways to leverage whatever they have to maximize financial or other equitable returns. This sometimes means advertising, and at other times, changing the playing field to suit their returns on investments (ROIs) better.

How can we grow and extend our organic reach to our stakeholders of media, partners, customers, and prospects, without an over–reliance on singular social networks? Think like a media owner.

Many years ago, I was interviewed by a media as a subject matter expert and subsequently put up the news clip on my website. After a few months, I was told to remove the clip, and asked to pay a rather large "fee." I understand their business decision, even though there was no financial consideration paid to me as an expert, nor was there a mutually signed waiver of rights beforehand, and worse, they could have informed me to remove the clip right after they saw it (rather than waited few months of "observation" as they mentioned).

Nonetheless, after that incident, I no longer put up any clips even though I am the content owner to my intellectual expertise, and from then only grant interviews where I explicitly retain ownership to my expressed expert perspectives.

After that incident, I generated my own content on my own Web properties to share with my customers and partners. It is a direct relationship I treasure, just as media owners treasure their direct relationships with their users.

In the same vein, businesses need to retain ownership of their precious content, however trivial it may seem. I am not talking about litigation. I am specifically talking about creating content of your own, and propagating it from your own means.

Think and act like a media owner, thereby casting your net wider and deeper. Learn from the best of the large media conglomerates. Many large media companies have succeeded in retaining control of their ever–growing content, without being constrained by the rules of technology providers.

Study your customers. Rather than simply trail the hype of developing native mobile apps, you can develop Web apps that are mobile–friendly, and save resources for other marketing expenditure. Most apps that streams updated information requires a "live" Internet connection, whether through 3G or WIFI. Media and commercial companies have discovered that often, a Web app works just as well as a native app, especially since content has to be retrieved online anyway.

Everything boils down to content. What are we offering to our customers, users and other stakeholders? What can we do better to create content? How can we extend the organic outreach of our content?

There are many ways, from the good old–fashioned good useful written content (always required), to the more audiovisual content such as mobile and Web video channels.

Audio–only content may have taken a dip, in densely populated areas where long road trips are replaced by darting in and out of metro subways, buses and taxis. So when creating video content, make the audio channels within the video useful as well, whether our users choose to view and listen, or just listen.

Build up Web properties that we post such audio, visual and textual content often. Business owners can start up with simple blogs (textual content, in conjunction with their corporate websites). It is not enough to have a few posts and hope for the best. We need a disciplined, well–studied, socially–conscious content team to make such posts grow, and in turn, endear and enlarge our user base.

It won't be an easy road to success as with all good things, but the efforts will pay off when we keep at it long and good enough, as we leave behind competitors who cannot keep up with the content marathon in a knowledge–driven economy. The road is long, you want to reach the end ahead of your competition. Keep running, keep learning, keep sharing.

Is fear the fuel for your social media adoption?

Any adoption of technology or marketing tactics should be founded on sound reasoning and projected returns on investment. What drives your social media adoption?

When we converse with families, friends, or peers, one of the common reasons for adopting technology is fear – the fear of missing or losing out, or being left behind. That may explain why some people glue their time on social media to feel attached to the people and the environment without a sense of losing out. There are also some commentaries which purport that those without a social media presence may seem "suspicious" to others. That may be stretching things too far, but such a perception cannot be ignored.

All these can raise an interesting point. This is because for someone who straddles between marketing and human resource development, I would certainly feel more comfortable if I know at least some cursory details about a candidate (for a job) or a potential client (for a business relationship). To find out about someone or some entity, the easiest point of entry is to search through the Internet, or explore the person or entity's social media presence.

Likewise, in our course of conversations with prospects and clients, it would appear that many would talk about social media adoption not from a fundamental and strategic need for social media to form their marketing, but rather from a fear of "losing out." The trouble with fear as the driving force is that the delivery of any social media campaign (sustained or blitz), may not be the best reason to go forward with.

Let me use martial arts as an analogy. Martial arts is a strict discipline, whether it be Muay Thai, Karate, Taekwondo, Shaolin, and so on. To attain growth and development in one's own martial art skills, it is important to not just have discipline, but to develop courage, benevolence and humility.

A great martial artist is never centered on fear or hatred, but is centered on compassion and humility, with a deep reverence for life and health.

Therefore, in the same light, any marketing strategy must be founded on reaching out to people in the right way, and never from fear of losing out, or hatred for market competition. The world is small, but sufficiently big enough to contain competitors to offer variance and vibrancy.

When you are deciding to move forward your social media channels, or to rejuvenate existing ones, remember to see how they fit in your overall marketing campaigns. It should start from a center of positivity and strength.

Huge Web graphics choking your online marketing?

Yes, bandwidth has skyrocketed in availability and become reasonable in costs, but that doesn't mean a developer should design and build Web files that are huge and silly. Build Web files that are compact and easy to download, and you win.

Files that are unnecessarily large are unfriendly to end–users, unfriendly to the development cycle, unfriendly to bandwidth, and unfriendly to costs, especially if your customer tries to download from mobile devices on the road.

I still come across my fair share of creatives from large shops who would create HUGE files that are merely intended for the low–resolution Internet.

Conversely, those of us who were pioneers of digital publishing and interactive media in the late 1980s have used the Mac SE with 3.5–inch floppy disks to create super–optimized graphics, illustrations, page layout files, animations, and interactive multimedia, compacting and optimizing files down to fit on limited storage media. Those skills of image and file optimization were carried over through all our work, including advertising and graphic design, digital photography, social media, mobile apps, and next–generation Web.

Even today, files should still be rightsized, and not made huge for no good reason. Just because a photographic image is huge does not make it good. A great photographer can shoot with a smartphone, with the right composition, the right perspective, the right moment, the right lighting, and get a photograph that is infinitely better and more appreciated as art, than an image taken on the most expensive camera with huge RAW files. It is not about the tool. It is about the creativity and perspective of the artist or photographer.

Likewise, when designing for the Web, files need to be friendly for users downloading our files on their browsers, whether on a desktop, a tablet, or a smartphone.

Graphics and images meant for the Web are not supposed to be as large as a file meant for a glossy magazine – think screen resolution. There are many tools that are meant for the modern Web, especially HTML5 tools that write elegantly small files. If you only need basic animation, cascading style sheet (CSS) and HTML5 make a great combination toolset for developing simple interactive files meant for Web banners, Web advertising, and even widgets for more complex websites.

There is no need at all, to use esoteric tools with embedded multi–megabyte static graphics and images. It just belies a lack of understanding for the Web paradigm compared to the traditional print paradigm.

It is never too often to repeat – the Web is NOT the same as the print medium. Even then, the print medium demands a sensible optimization of the images and graphics rightsized for specific purposes.

Is your website "responsive"?

Websites are not going away. They are now the repository and the center of your information and the broadcast hub to all your social media channels. How then, would you design your websites for social and mobile audiences?

Way back in 1996, when we first started consulting for government and corporations to help launch their websites and host them on our servers, it was a tedious time when we designed websites with clean, elegant HTML code by hand, writing HTML line by line. There was no CSS (cascading style sheets), so everything was encased within the Web page code. We designed websites that were accessible to as many users as possible. It was our philosophy that the Web belonged to all, not just for a few – as with the founding principles of the honorable Sir Tim Berners Lee, the inventor of the World Wide Web.

Sir Tim Berners Lee created the first Web browser, the first Web page editor, and the first Web server software, all from one of the most elegantly designed operating systems, NeXTSTEP (the precursor to Apple's OS X).

And through the years, I stuck to writing Web pages by hand, using nothing more than BBEdit, a programmers' text editor. The code written was clean and human readable, unlike the code generated by some complex website authoring tools, most of which I purchased and tried, but did not like using them. All that changed when I was too busy to maintain websites by hand, and had to look for a new way to write Web pages and maintain them not as singular pages, but through a content management system (CMS).

 I studied the landscape of available CMS, and settled with WordPress, which is extensible and great for daily use. There are limitations with WordPress, as with any CMS, but there are always plugins to extend the functionality of the system.

The code is not as succinct as handwritten code, but with faster and redundant Web hosts these days, websites can be made to run fast enough. If more speed is desired, there is the cloud to provide more availability and more redundancy, such as Amazon Cloudfront/S3. I started using WordPress and plugins to create desktop and tablet–friendly websites while repurposing the content for smartphones.

After some time, I wanted to explore an even easier way to target the websites for any screen – whether desktops, tablets or smartphones. I began investigating "responsive" themes, which are themes that intelligently scales visual and textual content based on the target platforms, whether desktop, tablet, or smartphone.

More WordPress themes are redesigned to be "responsive," while newer themes are designed this way. You may have to drop some widgets you have used before, and streamline the design to be more readable in a vertical "long" format since the headers, textual and visual content, and widgets, will flow in a long single column for smartphones; or you can adapt your website to have less or no widgets, reducing the length of content your users have to scroll through on smartphones.

Design tweaks and some widget compromises are worth it when you appreciate the elegance of the responsive themes and less troubleshooting of the installation. If you have already decided to forego handwritten code or complex authoring tools and to jump on the CMS model for your website delivery, think "responsive," think mobile.

3 key points for raving fans and better SEO

Companies struggling with social media and websites may have been zooming in on an ever–changing quicksand.

Perhaps it works better to look at something else to engage customers instead. Ms Ekaterina Walter wrote an enlightening piece* on social media engagement with some observations, that social media fans may not be viewing business posts, thereby reducing the outreach altogether.

For one, it would appear that when content is not engaging, even as fan numbers seem to escalate, engagement may reduce drastically, simply because fans are capable of hiding or blocking your updates altogether.

I know because I have done the same, hiding or blocking blatantly pushy or irrelevant posts. So while a fan may not necessarily unsubscribe (or "unfriend"), the fan's reluctance in reading any or all of your posts means that this fan should not be counted in your analytics. As a social media technology and marketing consultant, I shoulder the burden of trying out any different tools and platforms so that I can better advise clients. It is not a pretty sight. Social media platforms come and go, and some keep changing the rules of the game that sometimes it feels like struggling in quicksand for many clients. We have little room to complain as consultants since it is our duty to help our clients rise above the quicksand. But it can be exhausting to users and clients alike. Some get a sense of fatigue and leave the social media game altogether.

After all, communicating with real people (families, friends and peers) can easily be done through phone calls and email – still two of the most accessible methods. Some marketers use automated platforms to post social media updates, with the hope of trickling updates to reduce content fatigue on social media platforms.

Even then, users can become fatigued when the reality is that many of these updates are nothing more than advertisements of products and services, and do not have "edutainment" value. Users know that these updates are not a real conversation between two real people, but merely a form of uni–casting (one–to–many broadcasting).

Since search engines do not have access to social media accounts, trying to integrate social media platforms with search engine optimization (SEO) becomes challenging if not impossible for many companies.

So if both social media and SEO do not necessarily bring improvements to our objectives, customer retention and engagement, how should our outreach strategy be?

1. **Focus** on one or two most important social media platforms and build consistently on them, for content development and user engagement. It is futile to attempt to target way too many platforms, as most companies are resource–strapped.

2. Instead of merely obsessing over SEO, **build** real content instead. Keep the content on your own Web properties relevant, educational, and entertaining. These self–hosted content can easily be shared on your social media platforms, and will have a real positive impact on your SEO as well.

3. **Refine** your own Web properties. These are platforms you own, and can develop with the rules of your own, without limitations imposed by others. You can build content, supporting technologies that may even include your own private social network capabilities, as well as backend capabilities such as databases that can leverage on your corporate communication and outreach to customers and prospects.

Develop your own websites first and continually, and then build other social media offerings. Never neglect your own foundation and your own content fortress – your own website.

* http://www.fastcompany.com/3001871/your–facebook–fans–are–hiding–your–posts–alarming–rate

Fans, friends, or what?

In their eagerness to pursue the social network rush, clients often press for more "fans" or "friends" in their social network communities, imagining these to be equivalent to a business win. What are "fans" and "friends" really, in the context of branding and marketing?

The phenomenon of social networks is very similar to the dot–com boom just a decade ago. We cannot deny the surge in interest, adoption, and commercialization of social networks as a current mainstay of marketing and branding, just as corporations began to adopt "brochureware" websites when the Internet became commercialized in the 1990s.

However, it is important to understand the subtlety of the meaning of social networks when it comes to branding and marketing.

First, the notion of "friendship" on social networks is very different from a real–life friendship.

Real–life friendship is often distilled through a long time, and very few true friends will remain (sometimes none at all). But those true friends who remain will be people you are willing to trust, and vice versa. More likely than not, in times of difficulty, true friends will tend to your needs and care for you. True friends are people you want to spend time with. The older we are, the more likely we intend to spend as much time with such true friends as we physically can. Nothing beats having a few good friends over, sit down and enjoy deep and long conversations, over some pastries and tea (or coffee).

However, "friends" on a social network account may be people we may never have met, may never meet, and may not want to meet in real life. In some social network platforms, one has to be a "friend" or a "fan" of your page in order to read your writings, access certain privileged information, and even just to criticize or chastise you.

The "incentivization" with contests and rewards on social networks also blur the lines of such "friendship." The "friendship" in such a scenario becomes very different from a real–life friend.

Therefore, are many of these people fans, or friends at all?

Increasingly, there are new measurements to gauge how much of a "friend" a person is to our social network communities, including the use of the amount of engagement such a person has with our group. This is of course a good measurement of how intense or committed such a person is to communicating with our group (positively or negatively).

But we need not lose sleep over such transient online relations compared to our real lives. Let us remember it is yet another channel of communication, akin to the mainstream media.

When social networks fade away in the future (and they will, just as any technology has been in the past), some other medium may replace them. We simply adapt to whatever new channel rolls along, and study or adopt new communication channels judiciously and efficiently.

Different social media tools for different uses

How are you using various social media platforms? Do you use all the tools to show the same content? Or would you like to maximize the benefits and strengths of each platform?

Let's assume you have a self–hosted website that has great editorial content, with image galleries and other audiovisual content in a meticulously managed content management system (CMS). You maintain a YouTube channel for videos to allow your stakeholders to view and comment. You also keep a Twitter account, a LinkedIn page, and a Facebook fan page.

Rather than replicating the content from your website to your Twitter and Facebook fan page, which would simply turn your social media channels into mere "replicant" feeds, you could use each social media channel to your maximum benefit.

For example, your fan page can be a highly engaging social media channel to feature apps for promotions and contests. The wall can be a great place for your stakeholders to share and chat. Likewise, your Twitter thread can be a great and speedy place for your stakeholders to share short spurts of inspiration, links of interest, or to engage each other succinctly. Your LinkedIn page can be a place to interact with likeminded professionals for business partnerships and human capital.

Learn the benefits and strengths of each social media tool. Each of them present a plate of its own specialty, and can be used to bolster your social marketing campaigns in complementary, rather than replicated ways.

Blogging your way to social media success

According to an insightful article in Inc. Magazine (April 2012 issue), business blogging is in decline (from 2010 to 2011), compared to the slow but steady growth of businesses on social media channels such as Facebook and Twitter. Does that mean businesses no longer need to bother with blogging?

No. The reason is that while Twitter is great for short updates, and Facebook or Google+ offering opportunities for building real–time communities, blogging is a social media channel that you host, and the content you create, you own.

When you set up a self–hosted blog on platforms such as WordPress with a properly configured extended plug–in architecture, your content may be streamed automatically to your social media channels on a scheduled or real–time basis.

You can expound deep insights with illustrations, diagrams, images and multimedia on your blog, and have excerpts streamed automatically to your social media channels for your growing communities to pick up and digest as they wish.

No doubt, blogging takes effort and time, and requires a business to assign advocates and specialist writers to keep at it. It is not something you would assign to a person who has no interest in writing and research, or worse, no patience and discipline. This platform requires you to find the best candidates to front it and to keep at it. The rewards will come later, through establishing business expertise in the marketplace. It will take time, and effort. Don't give up!

Analytics? Useful, but don't go overboard

Every marketer or client seem to dive into analytics these days. But to what extent should we lean on analytics?

Every conceivable marketing mechanism, whether old school (such as print advertising) or the "latest and greatest" social media platforms, seem to present some kind of analytics for marketers to draw conclusions from.

Analytics are an easy data system to present to top management in place of perhaps more studied research. After all, without analytics, marketers may find it difficult to justify their expenditure to their bosses, who demand hard facts and figures, and who in turn, are pressured by stakeholders of all kinds to put facts and figures on the table (especially public listed entities).

Don't get me wrong, analytics to a certain degree are necessary, especially if they are derived from logical and field–tested assumptions and acquisition methods. With well–defined formulae and laboriously and properly derived statistics, analytics can be useful.

The trouble begins when someone relies on analytics as a crutch to counter objections from anyone on their marketing campaigns and programs, or to use as a plausible defense. It should not be, and realistically, cannot be.

Let us think of analytics from another perspective. Some of the greatest and most viral campaigns and programs did not really need to rely on analytics to prove any point.

One amazing phenomenon was Psy, the South Korean rapper and singer who shot to fame with his Gangnam Style song and dance routine. His music video variants became some of the most watched online around the world, and even inspired many people to create parody videos of the song and dance.

Did Psy's success needed analytics to prove a point? No. His wildly successful music video surpassed the necessity to prove its success with mere numbers. His song was launched in July 2012, and by early December 2012, more than 900 million people watched his video, with the song reaching the top in music charts in more than 30 countries worldwide.

Psy is a more unusual personal brand phenomenon in this regard, but he is not alone in how viral campaigns can propel a brand to previously unimaginable heights.

For example, the wildly addictive game Angry Birds from Rovio, had a video (since Mar 22, 2012) to promote its game Angry Birds Space, and the video was watched by more than 12 million people on YouTube, but who's counting?

Another popular video came from British Heart Foundation, with the use of actor Vinnie Jones, in the "hands only CPR" campaign. Since the video was launched on Nov 18, 2012, the video was watched by more than 13,000 people by Dec 8, 2012.

So, rather than clinging onto mere numbers for reports, we as practitioners may inspire more by thinking hard about how best to create marketing campaigns that would go insanely viral, and by endearing to more people than we can imagine.

After all, marketing is supposed to be creative and fun. Less counting please. Keep the humor and fun up. Keep creating. Keep smiling.

3 ways to owning content like the big shops

Every now and then, there are news about competing offerings from the big contenders – such as between Amazon, Apple, and Google. What does it mean for businesses big and small?

Most of us have used Google Maps in one way or another, whether simply as end–users browsing online Web content or on our mobile phones, or as developers embedding map calls in websites or mobile apps.

But there is more map providers than just Google Maps. Apple recently launched their own maps in their new iOS, and now, Amazon has their own maps too. I applaud all these efforts from the big contenders – they are good for consumers like us, and increase possibilities for app and Web developers too.

The big contenders on the Web, social media, and mobile arenas, are not simply replicating functionality for the sake of it. It is about control, and ultimately, the potential to monetize something you own. If you own something, you have the freedom to use it however you want it. If you own something, you also have the freedom to allow the free use of it, to lease it out, or to sell it altogether.

The same paradigm applies to why these big contenders, used here as an analogy, would have a functionality recreated that someone else already has.

Therefore, what does it mean for other businesses, including smaller businesses such as ours? Plenty.

Every now and then, we come face to face with a client who would question, "Why should we create our own content, or run our own Web properties? Why can't we simply post some content on social media sites?"

The same reason applies. The social media platforms are not owned by these clients, and the rules of engagement can change anytime, and more often than not, the rules have changed, and often not necessarily for the better for the clients.

Therefore, owning your own content is necessary, albeit requiring much more work from you, and from agencies like ours. There is no immediate returns to creating and developing content for you, since building content requires time, research, resources, and patience.

For enlightened clients, they recognize that engaging their customers require hard work and effort, but the fruits of labor will invariably endear their brands, products and services to their customers. The results are not immediate like the direct sale of a product, but are slowly built up through goodwill, trust, confidence, and sharing.

Here are some suggestions for content that a business can create:

1. **Textual content**. The most resource–friendly way to start is with a text blog, coupled with social media. Have internal employees write useful textual content, or work with an outsourced agency, to present editorially sound, and readable blogs. As the blogs become more developed, images and other multimedia resources can be included.

2. **Video content**. Video is not as easy to start as a text blog, but are much more compelling to end–users than lines and lines of text. With interesting videos, end–users will visit, and revisit your online presence, and will share the video content with others, and even share and post to social media, invariably increasing your outreach for you in a most viral way. Video can be simple videos from smartphones of your designated employees, or properly put together videos through a dedicated video and news production team.

3. **Interactive content**. Video and textual content you write on your blogs can allow comments from your customers, the most basic of interactive content. You can also create polls and questionnaires, where some commercial platforms even provide analytics you can use. If you are more ambitious, work with an outsourced agency to develop interactive games, simulations, puzzles, and even mobile and Web apps that put your interactive content onto desktop, tablet and even mobile devices. Interactive content demands commitment and resources, but are very engaging when done right, and will excite, attract end–users, and can go very viral.

Remember that big contenders were once small. Remember that every fruition requires hard work and committed resources, and don't come easy or free. Every business has a real opportunity for success.

Mobile, Video & Audio

Your own private mobile app "store"

Mobile apps is one of the fastest growing industries these days. Everyone with a smartphone (iOS, Android, Blackberry, Nokia) is likely to have downloaded an app or more from the respective mobile app repositories.

While there are millions of mobile apps publicly available for every purpose, there is also a trend for companies to design and deploy their own internal mobile apps. These apps contain proprietary and confidential information and are only to be used by their own internal employees, or trusted partners.

Therefore, such apps cannot be found on public app repositories. According to Fortune magazine, large multinational corporations such as IBM, General Electric and Genentech are all having their own internal app repositories.

Let us assume you run a typical large multinational corporation with people in research, in marketing, in manufacturing, in quality control, in logistics, and so on. There can be mobile apps that target particular management functions as well as apps for all employees, tapping on internal product knowledge to serve customers better.

The beauty of such internal app repositories is that you retain complete control on the apps, the devices that use the apps, with security and audit trails.

Augmented reality and QR codes for marketers

QR Codes are everywhere. You find them on billboards, posters, shopfronts, websites, magazines, and so on. They are simple to create and simple to use for consumers. So why do marketers need to look beyond ... soon?

QR Codes are simple, similar to barcodes you find on product packaging in supermarkets and the like. They can contain a single piece of information and typically, marketers would embed a website link within. The link can be a website, a microsite, a social media link, and so on. The advantage in this side of the world is that QR Codes are common, and consumers understand them. The smartphone penetration rate in Asia is very high, especially in highly populated and developed metropolitan cities and states. The broadband and 3G connections are also increasingly common in Asia, with places such as South Korea, Japan, and Singapore being some of the leading 3G (and beyond) locations.

With the backdrop of smartphone availability and broadband and cellular connectivity, marketers can easily leverage on the technological platforms to go beyond the QR Code.

We are talking about augmented reality.

There are many emerging vendors providing augmented reality technologies for marketers and content developers, including the likes of Layar (layar.com), Junaio (junaio.com), Argon (argon.gatech.edu), Wikitude (wikitude.com), Mixare (mixare.org), and many others.

Some are commercial offerings, and others, open source. Try them out to determine how each platform can work for your marketing efforts. We have tested the offering from Layar, which is a nicely developed platform that is very easy to create augmented reality content.

Assuming you have a print advertisement in a magazine, you can take the source file of the print advertisement and embed markers on the page, including videos (e.g. from your YouTube channel), website links, click–to–call, and so on. Layar works almost like a very simplified, script–less, stack–based authoring system reminiscent of HyperCard or SuperCard that I used in the eighties.

If you have already tried and deployed QR Codes for your marketing efforts, try augmented reality, and perhaps you can immerse your customers with a more engaging experience.

Videos the way forward in user engagement

I have been in public relations since the early nineties, and the general observation was this industry was glacial in evolution.

However, that has changed dramatically in recent years, with social media and mobile platforms erupting and forever changing how we communicate. I read a good article* which talked about video driving sales forward for some fast–moving consumer goods (FMCG) brands.

That was not surprising, as we have been working with video as a media and communications platform since the early days of desktop video and editing (remember AVID MSP and Adobe Premiere 1.0?) Some of us have also done broadcast journalism as foreign correspondents, as well as voiceover talents.

The challenge this side of the world is that not that many clients have yet warmed up to explore and exploit the use of digital video as a marketing and publicity tool. Video is powerful, and engages users so much more powerfully compared to audio podcasts, or just textual content.

Do a simple search online, and it is not difficult to find commercial research that points to the effectiveness of video as a communications tool compared to audio and mere text. Even traditional media has embraced video of some kind.

Just look at the mainstream newspapers in Asia, and you can find their online versions with some video content. Some even have dedicated video crew, facilities and studios to develop video news content.

Therefore, from the client–side, and especially from our end as publicists, the need to push for video news content is critical.

The barrier to entry for video news production has come down tremendously. When we used AVID Media Suite Pro, the lowest end product of the AVID desktop video editors, it was around US$10,000+, not counting the rather expensive Mac platform then, and video footage acquisition equipment like cameras, tape decks, audio interfaces, and so on.

Today, you can edit simple video news content with nothing more than iMovie or Final Cut Pro X, and video cameras have also come down in costs while scaling up in quality.

The good thing about video news content is that it is not about making flashy TV commercials or special effects (those might be scorned at by the media), but good factual documentaries or snippets. The content is more important than fancy embellishments, which do not add value to news.

The typical video news content can be executive interviews, with questions and answers, or some brief product previews. If the client is enlightened, more in–depth video developments can be built on, including custom scripting, storytelling, film development, with professional casting and crew to make the production a powerful, engaging, "film–like" communications product that would attract viewers and customers.

* http://www.emarketer.com/Article.aspx?R=1009290

The camera does not make the photographer

If you love photography, it is about bringing your perspective to others. It is not about how expensive your gear is. I read an article by William Porter* which resonated deeply with me.

Photography is really about capturing a moment or an image in time, and not about megapixels, f–stops, price, brands, etc.

I have been dabbling in photography since my teens. I have used a Minolta SLR in the early days with a single prime lens. When I started working, an old professional photographer introduced me to medium–format photography – by selling me his old Mamiyaflex C220 TLR. That TLR changed my entire view of photography, and I managed to use that to shoot professional–quality portraiture and nature on 120 film, and I absolutely loved it. The suspense of shooting a whole roll of film and then anticipating the outcome, was what made photography magical for me.

Then life caught up with me, and I lost touch with photography. But photography is really part of the genetic makeup of me, being a creative and a designer at heart. Eventually, the digital revolution came, and film photography was slowly and steadily eroded by digital photography. I too, took the plunge. I bought many cameras along the way, and went from compact cameras to chunky DSLRs alike. But it was difficult to find a camera that really suited my needs.

I am getting on with age, and with time, heavy and chunky DSLRs that are also very expensive, do not appeal to me. As a publicist, and sometimes journalist, I need a nimble camera that can easily capture precious moments or images on time, with little fuss, with good image quality, that do not depend on sheer muscle to lift or move the camera, or even stable hands or pristine eyesight to capture decent images.

Recently, I found the Olympus OM–D EM–5, a digital remake of Olympus' own OM film cameras, with the same classic look and feel, and equipped with great image stabilization technology. Although "merely" a micro 4/3 (MFT) camera with a sensor much smaller than a full–frame 35mm sensor or even an APS–C sensor, the OM–D is great when you need images captured fast, with good image quality that rivals some DSLRs, and is light enough to bring around, with plenty of lenses to choose from.

Technology moves so fast that even stalwarts like Leica are wising up to the modern era, with the recent launch of their new M and M–E, catering to HD video needs and smaller price tags. The competition is fierce. You have Fuji, Sony and other makers clamoring for the same field, and DSLR stalwarts like Canon and Nikon flooding the market with appropriate wares that cater to their audiences as well. It is a crowded space with ever–improving image capture, stabilization, video and extensibility functions.

Put a samurai sword in the hands of a young child, and the outcome is disastrous. The tool complements the artist, and the tool does not make the artist.

It is about perspective. Put a US$30,000 camera in the hands of a person with no aesthetic feel, and you can get boring, uninspired (albeit sharp) images.

Put even a simple smartphone in the hands of a professional photographer and artist, and you can get inspiring images. Top fashion photographer Chuck Jackson proved that inspiringly with just a phone.

Choose a camera that suits your practical needs, congruent with your desired outputs, budget, and state of health. Start capturing the precious moments and images in time. That is what really matters.

* http://www.techhive.com/article/1167690/do– you–really–need–a–dslr.html

How to use Mobile Apps for Marketing

Some marketing folks were interviewed in a magazine on why mobile apps did not get the thumbs up as a marketing tool.

Those interviewed felt many mobile apps are "me too" replicants, with way too many advertisements or sales messages, and are often measured by top management merely by downloads or monetization. And yet, every business leader seems to insist on having an app for his business, whether or not his business needs it or not.

Remember when the Internet became commercial and companies could register their own .COM domains? It quickly became a frenzy of domain registrations. Then when Flash came along, every company dumped the good old HTML code and went full force into dizzying animated websites. The same phenomenon is happening to the mobile app space today.

However, just because everyone's having an app does not mean we can't have one of our own. The real trick is to understand what it does for us.

1. The app can be a simple **content tool** that your customers and stakeholders can read on the road in a pocketable device. That's where the news feed and your short posts on social media channels become "live" through the mobile app.

2. Make the app **interactive** with your customers. The simplest is to allow comments through your mobile app, either through built-in commenting systems, or by integrating with

your social media channels. You can also embed polls, surveys, events, promotions, and complex social games to attract your customers and prospects to continue to interact with you through your mobile app. Your customers can share your content and build "word of mouth" if they feel like it.

3. Think of your app as a **social** networking microcosm, rather than imagining it as an advertising medium to hawk your wares. The fastest way to lose your customers on your mobile app is to hawk your wares relentlessly.

4. The mobile app **should not simply be measured** as successful based on the number of downloads, or having ad banners ad nauseam. Again, go back to the first premise, that the mobile app can be a content repository, a light-hearted place of entertainment, and mostly, a place to interact with people.

Make the app content–rich (which is probably the easiest), or entertaining (in a game format, but need more time and investment), and people will want to download it, use it, and keep it. The mobile app is no longer restricted to a single popular platform these days. You can even use a well-written HTML5 code and target just about any smartphone platform today without the need for a native app. You have choices.

So the options are much wider for you, and the costs of design and implementation are coming down. What are you waiting for?

Smartphone video journalism for everyone

Someone once said the best camera is the one with you. I agree. There are many advanced professional cameras in the market, but all too often, the perfect video or still photographic opportunity slips away from us because we did not have a camera with us. Or did we?

DSLRs, especially full frame ones, are great for image quality, have tons of accessories, but are extremely heavy to lug around, and use it continuously for the average person. Not all of us are professional photographers, nor do we want to. If you are, like me, into using the DSLR for HD videography, then using a heavy DSLR for video is even more strenuous then using the DSLR for stills.

Therefore, if we are into seizing the video (or still) opportunity whenever or wherever we may be, then the only camera we often carry with us, is our smartphone.

You may be using an iOS, Android, or Windows smartphone. Any smartphone with a good quality camera is the one you want, especially if it comes with good video and still photography features. Software–based effects are not important, because we are talking about video journalism, not special effects. If you are still in the market looking for the best smartphone for mobile videography, the Nokia Lumia 920 is a smartphone with great optical qualities, including image stabilization. You can also attach an external microphone for better audio capture. You can also use some Android or iOS smartphones with good optics. It is not about the megapixels alone. Look closely at how well the optics perform in a variety of lighting conditions, whether under bright sunlight, dim lighting, moving objects, backlight situations, and other common video or photographic challenges.

Next, remember to hold the camera horizontally. All too often, I have seen videos captured in the vertical format, which is incompatible with how videos should be – horizontal. It is all right to hold your smartphone upright if you are shooting stills, such as portraiture. But if you are into video journalism, please remember to hold your smartphone horizontally. You haven't seen TV images "tall" have you?

Holding a smartphone momentarily just to snap a still image is easy. But holding it horizontally to shoot a longer video feature, becomes a bit uncomfortable over time. It is easier to treat your smartphone as a video camera, and mount it either on a tripod, or with a rig. There are small as well as elaborate adapters which can mount your smartphone onto tripods.

There are stabilizer rigs that would make your smartphone behave like a "steady–cam"–like camera, or handheld rigs that simply allow you to hold your smartphone more like how you would hold a boom microphone. Any stabilizer that allows you to hold your smartphone more ergonomically to use it over extended periods of time, is better than trying to hold it with your fingers alone.

Most smartphones do not have optical zoom lenses, or detachable lenses. They usually have a wide–angle fixed lens, with less than ideal depth of field (DOF). This means that your videos will not approximate the kind you can achieve with a high–end video camera with shallow DOF lenses, or even an HD DSLR with detachable prime lenses with great f–stops to achieve that shallow DOF effect. But all is not lost. You can attach third–party optics to your smartphone, giving it telephoto or even macro capabilities (at the expense of bulk and size of course).

Otherwise, observe old–school video and still photography values: Walk closer to an object or subject if you want to "zoom closer," and walk farther away if you want to have a wider view. Do also remember that most smartphones have wide–angle lenses, which means you have to go very close to a person to get a close–up or extreme close–up view, and invariably, distorting the features of the face. In such scenarios, see if you can invest in add–on telephoto lenses to allow you to film further from your subject.

Audio recording on a smartphone, especially from a distance, will be usually noisy, even though some smartphones feature noise–isolation features for voice calls. In such instances, attach third–party external microphones through the 3.5mm audio jack of your smartphone. If you can, use a wired powered microphone for video interviews, since the microphone can be held as close to your subject as possible, akin to how ENG broadcast journalists record their sounds. If you cannot use a wired microphone, find a third–party "shotgun" microphone, and mount it on your smartphone or get a small rig to mount the shotgun microphone on it with your smartphone. The setup won't be as small as a mere smartphone, but the setup will allow you to capture better quality audio and offer you the option of a more stable camera setup as well.

Generally, even with all the equipment you need to lug around with a smartphone as the primary imaging device, you will still be carrying much less than someone who has to carry a large HD DSLR or video camera. This offers you, the mobile video journalist or communication professional, every opportunity to grab an interview, to upload to your social media and online video channels very quickly. That is sometimes, the difference between a real news scoop, versus a "me too" segment that trails the others.

If you think that great cinematography is a byproduct only of expensive cameras, think again.

Director Hooman Khalili hacked together the Nokia N8 to shoot an indie feature film "Olive" (olivethemovie.com).

Great cinematography is about a great story, and how it is beautifully told from the heart. May your journey in video journalism be amazing and fruitful!

dot zen 2.0

248

Author & Contributor

Seamus Phan

26+ years in marketing, technology (digital media, publishing, content management and Internet), and business strategy. Authored books on technology, marketing, service quality, and total quality. He was an inductee of the 500 Profiles in Excellence, amongst the likes of Nobel Peace Prize winner President Kim Dae–Jung, artist Peter Gabriel, movie director Jean–Jacques Annaud, Cardinal Jan Peer Schotte (Sec–Gen of the World Synod of Bishops), the Barons 500 Leaders of the New Century, alongside the likes of Sir Arthur C Clarke and Bill Gates. As a journalist, he has co–hosted international TV and radio segments, and written for international and technical, business, health, and branding media. Editorial judge (Tabbies). Featured as "Brainstormer" in Seth Godin's "BullMarket 2004". He earned a doctoral degree in Business. He had conducted graduate–level research in the areas of autoxidation of lipids in his younger years. http://SeamusPhan.com.

Ter Hui Peng

22+ years in media and publishing industry. Hui Peng has worked in the media industry since 1991, having been regional manager for Asian Business Press (later Miller Freeman before renamed as CMP Media). She now leads the PR practice of McGallen & Bolden. She has deep industry experience in the entire spectrum of marketing, including high–tech marketing, Internet content management, publicity, public relations (PR), training and development, direct marketing, seminar and event management. She has consulted on retainer and projects for hundreds of high–tech, biotech, medical, consumer (FMCG), lifestyle, and other clients, including bestselling authors, leading branding and management consultants. She teaches media training camps and other publicity programs. She earned a Masters degree in Training and Development (Leicester). Co–author of the original DotZen book with Seamus Phan.

Like to learn more?

Like to build your business through holistic marketing,
public relations, social and mobile media, and human capital?

Contact us at **www.mcgallen.com**.